# SHIP SPOTTER'S GUIDE

OSPREY
PUBLISHING

# SHIP SPOTTER'S GUIDE

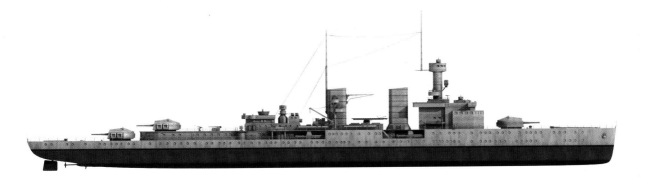

Compiled by Angus Konstam

First published in Great Britain in 2014 by Osprey Publishing,
PO Box 883, Oxford, OX1 9PL, UK
PO Box 3985, New York, NY 10185-3985, USA
E-mail: info@ospreypublishing.com

Osprey Publishing is part of the Osprey Group
© 2014 Osprey Publishing

Every attempt has been made by the Publisher to secure the appropriate permissions for material reproduced in this book. If there has been any oversight we will be happy to rectify the situation and written submission should be made to the Publishers.

Angus Konstam has asserted his right under the Copyright, Designs and Patents Act, 1988, to be identified as the compiler and editor of this work.

Artwork by Tony Bryan, Peter Bull, Hugh Johnson, Steve Noon, Ian Palmer, Guiseppe Rava, Wayne Reynolds and Paul Wright.

A CIP catalogue record for this book is available from the British Library

ISBN: 978 1 4728 0869 1
PDF ISBN: 978 1 4728 0870 7
Epub ISBN: 978 1 4728 0871 4

Typeset in ConduitITCStd and Cambria
Originated by PDQ Digital Media Solutions, Suffolk
Printed in China through Worldprint Ltd.

14 15 16 17 18   10 9 8 7 6 5 4 3 2 1

Osprey Publishing is supporting the Woodland Trust, the UK's leading woodland conservation charity, by funding the dedication of trees.

Editor's note: All material in this book is drawn from previous publications in Osprey's New Vanguard series. All measurements are approximate. Detailed ship plans were only produced from the 17th century onwards, so some of the specifications listed here for earlier warships are approximate, based on the latest historical and archaeological research.

**www.ospreypublishing.com**

### CONVERSION TABLE

| | |
|---|---|
| 1 millimetre (mm) | 0.0394in |
| 1 centimetre (cm) | 0.3937in |
| 1 metre (m) | 1.0936 yards |
| 1 kilometre (km) | 0.6214 miles |
| 1 kilogram (kg) | 2.2046 lb |
| 1 inch (in) | 2.54cm |
| 1 foot (ft) | 0.3048m |
| 1 yard | 0.9144m |
| 1 mile | 1.609km |

# CONTENTS

# INTRODUCTION

**W**arships have existed almost as long as mankind has plied the seas. The first recorded warships date from more than 3,000 years ago, and while their appearance has changed markedly, the role of these ships has largely remained unchanged. In their simplest and oldest role, warships exist to protect the sea lanes, and to safeguard friendly ships. How this is achieved can vary enormously. In the Ancient World, it meant keeping the seas free of pirates and maintaining a fleet to counter an attack by enemy squadrons. In the great 'Age of Fighting Sail' warships had become more specialized, and so the job of protecting the sea lanes was carried out by smaller warships, while the larger ones – the ships-of-the-line – stood ready to fight the enemy for control of the seas.

The advent of steam and steel did little to alter this basic role, or change the division of functions. If anything, warships became even more divided by form and function. In theory the advent of the ironclad rendered all existing warships obsolete, but wooden-hulled ships still had a role to play as commerce raiders or as patrol vessels, gunboats or pirate hunters. The next great revolution came in 1905, with the launch of HMS *Dreadnought*. For the second time in half a century existing warships were rendered obsolete, and so a new arms race began – one that arguably was instrumental in the increase of diplomatic tension that led to the outbreak of World War I.

In that 'war to end all wars', the great fleets of dreadnoughts faced each other across the North Sea, while other smaller ships established the blockade of Germany and cleared the sea lanes of German shipping. Ultimately the great clash of dreadnoughts at Jutland in 1916 did less to bring about the end of the war than the hardships created by the Allied blockade. The German response was to launch their U-boats against Allied shipping. This led to a new kind of warfare – or rather a more modern version of the commerce raiding and privateering of previous centuries. The war also saw the emergence of naval airpower and the creation of the first aircraft carriers.

By 1942 it was clear that aircraft carriers rather than battleships were now the arbiters of victory at sea. Submarines too had a greater role in World War II than in the previous global conflict, although they also demonstrated their vulnerability to new forms of anti-submarine warfare.

Since the end of World War II, submarines and aircraft carriers have continued to reign supreme. While the end of the Cold War removed the need for large fleets of nuclear submarines, the new breed of super carriers and cruise-missile armed surface ships and submarines have seen the old limits of sea power removed. Now, thanks to modern weaponry, naval task forces can make their presence felt thousands of miles from the sea. This more than anything demonstrates that warships are as useful today as they have ever been. Just as they have for centuries, warships protect maritime trade, and serve as a counterpoint to enemy naval aggression. The difference, though, is that today's warships have a global reach, and possess a degree of destructive potential unmatched in 3,000 years of naval history.

Angus Konstam
Orkney, 2014

# ANCIENT WARSHIPS

**M**ankind's long association with the sea began in the Neolithic period, around 12,000 years ago – the earliest date archaeologists have found evidence of maritime trade. However, the earliest known images of boats came much later, around 5,500 years ago, when crude vessels were first depicted in rock carvings and pottery found in the valley of the River Nile and in Greece. One of these Greek craft, dated around 3500 BC, possibly contains the first depiction of a warship and a naval battle. It shows a light oared vessel with an archer on its deck.

By around 2000 BC pictorial images of boats become more commonplace, but it was not until about 1200 BC that we first see the depiction of craft that are indisputably warships. These date from the reign of Pharaoh Ramses III (reigned 1186–1155 BC), and show slender-oared galleys, fitted with a single mast and sail. Images of these ships taking part in a great naval battle commemorate the pharaoh's victory over the Sea Peoples in c.1175 BC.

In the Aegean at around the same time, similar oared vessels appear on vase fragments and as votive models, and by the 8th century BC depictions of far more powerful Assyrian vessels appear – *biremes*, powered by two banks of oars. By the 6th century BC *biremes* are frequently depicted in Greek art, but by the end of the century they begin to be replaced by even larger *triremes*, with three overlapped oar banks. These evolved into the classic Greek *trireme* – the warships that triumphed over the Persians at the Battle of Salamis (480 BC) and which fought in the Peloponnesian War. By the 4th century BC four- and five-banked *quadriremes* and *quinquiremes* appear, and these became the primary warships in use during the First Punic War, fought between Carthage and Republican Rome. Roman naval supremacy in the Mediterranean basin rendered these great lumbering warships unnecessary, which led to a return to lighter but faster *biremes*, ideal for hunting down pirates. These remained in use until after the fall of the Roman Empire.

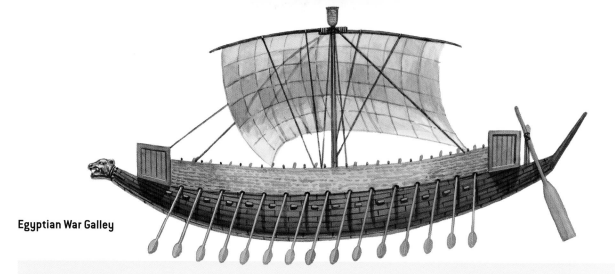

**Egyptian War Galley**

## SPECIFICATIONS: ATHENIAN TRIREME

**Length:** 36.80m (120ft)

**Beam (hull):** 3.65m (12ft)

**Beam (outriggers):** 5.45m (18ft)

**Draught:** 1.20m (4ft)

**Displacement:** 41.3 tons

**Crew total:** 200

**Oarsmen:** 170

62 upper oarsmen

54 middle oarsmen

54 lower oarsmen

**Armed men:** 14

10 citizen marines

4 mercenary archers

**Specialist seamen:** 16

1 sea captain

1 helmsman

1 bo'sun

1 bow officer

1 shipwright

1 double-pipe player

10 deck hands

**Athenian Trireme**

## Ship details

**Previous page:** This warship is based on the relief of Ramses III at Medinet Habu *c.*1175 BC. These ships were probably the pride of the Egyptian Navy and at the cutting edge of current technology. Though they bear similarities with earlier Egyptian vessels, the rigging, loose-footed sail, transverse beams strengthening the hull and simplified bow and stern decorations make them similar to those of other Mediterranean cultures.

**This page:** This artwork depicts an Athenian trireme. The fundamental innovation of a 5th century BC trireme was that the oarsmen were not arranged in straight lines, but in three staggered banks. This arrangement meant that the rowers didn't hamper each other, and there was no need for a high freeboard or an exceptionally long vessel.

# THE NORSE LONGSHIP

The earliest representation of Scandinavian ships date from the late Stone Age, around 2000 BC, while the first surviving vessel is the Hjortspring boat, built around 200 BC. This was a simple wooden dugout with built-up plank sides, which has been seen as the forerunner of the more developed Nydam and Kvalsund boats, whose remains date to the 4th and 7th centuries respectively. The style of the two is similar, but the latter vessel was designed to carry a mast and sail.

Two other finds made during the same period shed greater light on the craft used by Norse seafarers. In 1904 the Oseberg ship was found inside a ship burial mound near Oslo. It was powered by 15 oars a side. It was a high status pleasure vessel rather than a longship, and was built around AD 950. The Gokstad ship, also found during the excavation of a burial mound, was built a few decades earlier than the Oseberg vessel, and was both larger and sturdier.

Since then other Norse ships have been uncovered, most notably at Skuldelev in Denmark, where the remains of an 11th century longship was recovered. These, combined with pictorial references and descriptions from Norse sagas, have combined to give us a detailed understanding of how these vessels were built and what they looked like. They were long and narrow, and a typical longship would have 30 oars per side, manned by 60 oarsmen. When not under oars the vessel would be powered by a single mast and square sail, and steered by a steering oar set on the starboard quarter. With this number of men on board there was little room for storage, particularly as the vessel was ballasted with up to 6 tons of large stones to ensure she remained stable and trim. Despite their long length to breadth ratio, these vessels were highly manoeuvrable and just as well suited to short voyages across the North Sea or the Baltic as to sailing up rivers in search of settlements and plunder.

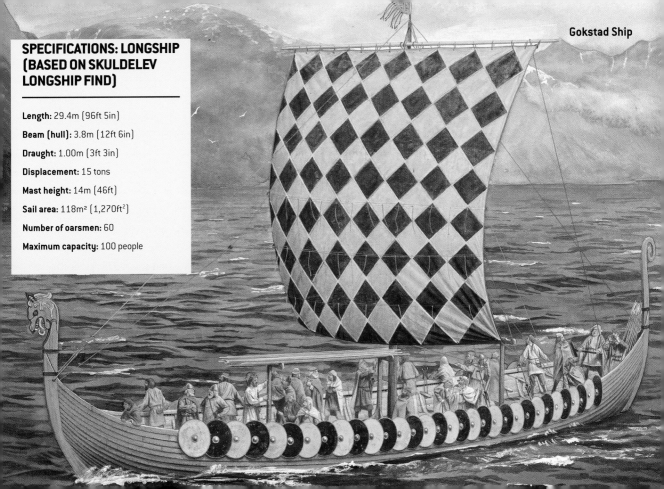

Gokstad Ship

## SPECIFICATIONS: LONGSHIP (BASED ON SKULDELEV LONGSHIP FIND)

**Length:** 29.4m (96ft 5in)

**Beam (hull):** 3.8m (12ft 6in)

**Draught:** 1.00m (3ft 3in)

**Displacement:** 15 tons

**Mast height:** 14m (46ft)

**Sail area:** 118m² (1,270ft²)

**Number of oarsmen:** 60

**Maximum capacity:** 100 people

**Knarr, 11th century AD**

## Ship details

**Previous page:** The Gokstad ship was found with 64 painted shields in situ, lining the sides of the hull as shown here, however, they wouldn't have remained there in any sort of rough weather. Although the original vessel lacked the elegantly carved stem and sternpost decoration shown here, contemporary images suggest that dragon carvings in the prow and curled stempost decorations were often used to augment a longship's appearance.

**This page:** An 11th century *knarr*, cargo carrying vessel or trade ship, as it would have appeared en route to Iceland. Note the exposed conditions that had to be endured on the long voyages by the crew and passengers alike. Most Viking ships of the era shared the same basic construction.

# WARSHIPS OF THE FAR EAST

The earliest surviving description of Oriental warships dates from 486 BC, but the details are scant. More information is obtained from sources from the Chinese Han Dynasty (202 BC–AD 220), when warships varied in size and function, from small oared rams to large oared 'battleships'. These large and prestigious warships, some of which were several decks high, remained in use for several centuries. However, it was the medieval period before China built large fleets of war junks. The Mongol Invasion Fleet sent to Japan in the late 13th century is well documented, and these vessels differed from their mercantile counterparts solely through their weaponry and function – not their general construction or appearance.

Japanese and Korean warships developed along slightly different lines. In Korea, the 'turtle ships' of the 15th century are an example of a specialist form of armoured warship, while in Japan warships tended to combine oar and sail power, but like the Chinese they merged the firepower provided by war engines mounted in the bows with the melee potential of well-armed marines. However, there was little technological development, and by the time the Chinese and Japanese came into contact with European explorers and merchants in the 16th century their vessels were distinctly inferior to the European designs. During the *Sengoku* ('Warring States') period in the 15th and 16th centuries, widespread conflict within Japan served as a catalyst for further naval development. One result of this was the *ataka bune*, a form of Japanese 'battleship' designed to serve as a fleet or squadron flagship. More common was the smaller *seki bune*, a box-like oar and sail-equipped fighting platform that formed the mainstay of *Sengoku*-era fleets. Both the Chinese and the Japanese made use of specialist warships too – vessels such as fast but lightly armed patrol craft, fireships, command ships and gun-armed warships were designed. However, the distinct lack of development in ship design meant the warships of Europe evolved at a significantly faster pace than those of the Far East, until the Oriental adoption of Western shipbuilding traditions in the late 19th century.

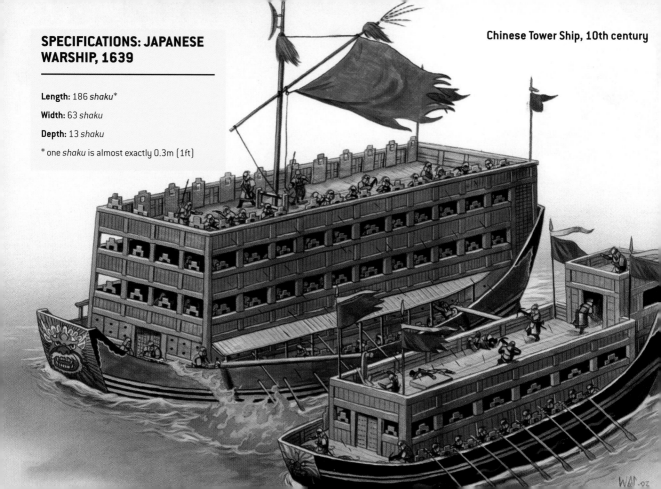

**SPECIFICATIONS: JAPANESE WARSHIP, 1639**

**Length:** 186 *shaku*\*

**Width:** 63 *shaku*

**Depth:** 13 *shaku*

\* one *shaku* is almost exactly 0.3m (1ft)

Chinese Tower Ship, 10th century

# Ship details

**Previous page:** Around AD 975 the Tangs built *lou chuan* (tower ship) vessels to use in their war against the rival Song dynasty. These classic Chinese 'battleships' were floating fortresses, their sides pierced with loopholes for crossbows and spears. Trebuchets on the upper deck provided even greater firepower, while doors in the hull allowed marines carried inside the vessel to attack and board enemy warships.

**This page:** Naval engagements were commonplace between rival clans during the *Sengoku* period, but a lack of technological progress meant that most warships conformed to standard designs. Here a large *ataka bune* attacks a smaller but more commonplace *seki bune*. Both vessels have a distinctly block-like appearance, and although they were sluggish and difficult to manoeuvre, they suited the Japanese style of fighting, where firepower was used to augment a vessel's boarding capabilities.

**Japanese warships, 16th century**

# TUDOR WARSHIPS

The seizure in 1485 of the English crown by Henry Tudor took place at a time of profound change in the design and function of sailing warships. This change spread across much of Western Europe, but the Tudors were quick to embrace new technological advances, and harnessed them to build a powerful royal fleet. The medieval cog of Northern Europe had evolved into the carrack through its amalgam with Mediterranean shipbuilding practices. Old clinker-built ships were replaced by ones with flush-fitting carvel-built hulls, whose smooth sides were better suited to the introduction of gun ports. This in turn came about due to new developments in the design of artillery, and the desire to mount these increasingly powerful guns in warships.

The result was the carrack, a type of vessel that was robust enough to handle the demands imposed by the deployment of guns on board, yet manoeuvrable enough to outperform most other vessels of the era. These carracks formed the core of Henry's royal fleet, a navy inherited by his son Henry VIII when he acceded to the throne in 1509. Supporting these large, powerful warships were an array of smaller vessels – galleys, galleasses and lighter despatch vessels and patrol ships. By the time Henry died in 1547 his fleet was one of the most powerful in Europe.

These ageing ships formed the core of his daughter Elizabeth I's fleet when she gained the throne in 1559. However, she was keen to embrace the latest changes in warship design and armament. The result was the introduction of the 'race-built galleon', a type of warship that was faster, sleeker and more manoeuvrable than the carrack, but which possessed an even more powerful and homogenous armament of heavy guns. The first of these royal warships appeared in 1573, and by the time of the Spanish Armada campaign of 1588 they constituted the powerful heart of a modern fleet. In fact many of these Elizabethan galleons were modernized during the 1580s, rendering them among the most powerful all-round warships of the period.

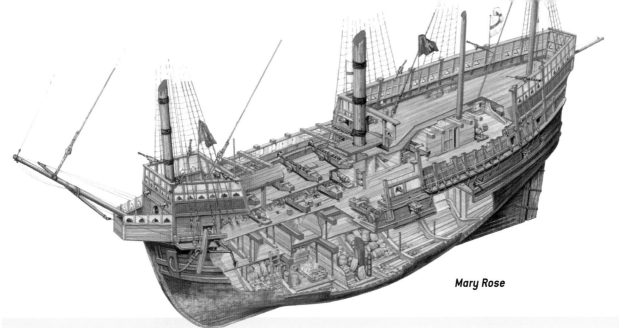

*Mary Rose*

## SPECIFICATIONS: *MARY ROSE*

**Built:** 1509/10 in Portsmouth

**Launched:** 1511

**Length (keel):** 32m (105ft)

**Beam:** 11.58m (38ft)

**Draught:** 4.57m (15ft)

**Displacement:** 500 tons (700 tons after 1536 refit)

**Armament:** 44x heavy guns, 16x swivel guns

**Crew (1512):** 400 (including 200 soldiers and 20 gunners)

**Fate:** Sunk, July 1545; raised in 1982 and now a museum ship.

## Ship details

**Previous page:** The *Mary Rose* was a carrack, built in Portsmouth in 1509–10. She was one of the first warships purpose-built to carry heavy ordnance, and she saw action off Brest in 1513. In 1536 she underwent an extensive refit, and more guns were added. This lowered her centre of gravity, a factor that contributed to her loss off Portsmouth in July 1545. Her remains were discovered in 1970, and she was finally raised in 1982.

**This page:** The small 250-ton *Swiftsure* was built in Deptford in 1573, and was one of the first of England's new race-built galleons, a ship type devised by Sir John Hawkins. When they entered service the *Swiftsure* and her sister ship *Dreadnought* were regarded as the fastest warships in the English fleet. Despite her small size, *Swiftsure* carried a respectable armament of 34 guns, weapons she used to good effect against the Spanish Armada.

*Swiftsure*

# THE SPANISH GALLEON

The ships of exploration used by Christopher Columbus were small carracks and carvels (small lateen-rigged sailing vessels). During the early 16th century these ship types gradually evolved and amalgamated to produce the galleon. The term first emerged during the 1520s and 1530s, when it referred to small warships used by the Spanish as patrol and escort vessels. The form these early galleons took is unclear, but by the 1560s they had developed into a characteristic type of vessel – one that would remain in use for more than a century. Typically a galleon of the late 16th century had a much leaner profile than earlier carracks, but was characterized by a high sterncastle. This was included to make the vessel a more commodious fighting platform, but it also acted like a sail, pushing the ship slightly to leeward as it moved through the water.

Galleons were usually well armed, with a combination of large guns and smaller swivel guns (or *versos*). However, unlike contemporary English ships, the Spanish used two-wheeled gun carriages rather than four-wheeled ones, which made the guns harder to run out or reload. This, though, was a reflection of Spanish practice; they aimed to fire their guns in one big broadside before boarding the enemy. They then relied on their superbly trained Spanish soldiers to win the day.

Spanish galleons were frequently used to protect the annual treasure fleets sailing between the New World and Spain, and by 1600 they had become the treasure carriers themselves as they had the ability to defend themselves if attacked. Treasure galleons formed the core of the Spanish Armada used to attack Elizabethan England in 1588. Its ultimate failure was due more to poor planning and bad luck than any significant inferiority of Spanish warships. The English also avoided being boarded and relied more on gunnery than the Spanish, which nullified the latter's advantage in close combat. The Spanish galleon remained in use well into the 17th century, by which time a new generation of warships replaced these floating symbols of Spanish power.

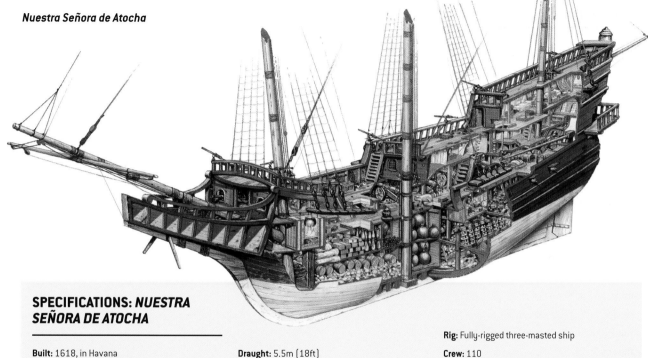

*Nuestra Señora de Atocha*

## SPECIFICATIONS: *NUESTRA SEÑORA DE ATOCHA*

**Built:** 1618, in Havana

**Length (keel):** 32m (105ft)

**Beam (hull):** 8.1m (26ft 7in)

**Draught:** 5.5m (18ft)

**Displacement:** 492 tons

**Armament:** 20x large bronze guns, 8x *versos*

**Rig:** Fully-rigged three-masted ship

**Crew:** 110

**Soldiers:** 90

**Fate:** Sunk in a hurricane, 1622

# Ship details

**Previous page:** The galleon *Nuestra Señora de Atocha* (Our Lady of Atocha) was built in Havana in 1618 for service in the treasure fleets. She was typical of the Spanish galleons of the early 17th century, although there were complaints that she was considerably less sturdy than galleons built in Spain. In 1622 she sank off the Florida Keys, when she was caught in a hurricane. Her remains were rediscovered in 1985.

**This page:** The 750-ton treasure galleon *San Juan de Bautista* was the *Almirante* (flagship) of the Castille Squadron during the Spanish Armada campaign of 1588. During the fighting she formed part of an elite ad hoc squadron composed of the most powerful galleons in the fleet, which was used to protect the rest of the armada from English attacks. Although badly battered she survived the campaign, and eventually limped back to Spain.

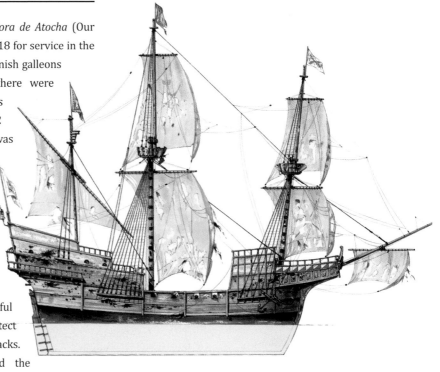

*San Juan de Bautista*

# WARSHIPS OF THE ANGLO-DUTCH WAR

The English and Dutch went to war three times during the 17th century, in 1652–54, 1665–67 and 1672–74. These wars were almost exclusively fought at sea, between two well-matched rival fleets. It was a time of transition in naval warfare, as new technology, improved shipbuilding methods and improved weaponry all had an impact on the way warships were designed and used. The ships of the two maritime rivals were similarly designed and built, with three important exceptions. Generally, English warships were more stoutly built than Dutch ones, with thicker beams and frames. This then allowed the English to add more guns to their vessels, often giving them a slight edge in a sea battle. Finally, the Dutch ships had shallower draughts than English vessels, allowing them to operate in the shallow coastal waters, estuaries and rivers of the Dutch coastline. That meant that when they reached home waters they were relatively safe from attack. However, above all, this was a time of tactical innovation.

During the First Dutch War (1652–54) battles tended to be scrappy affairs, where the ships intermingled with each other like an aerial dogfight of World War I. Towards the end of the war the English developed tactical guidelines, which made the most of their superior armament. From that point on they fought in long lines, so the enemy were presented with an unbroken line of guns; the Dutch adopted line-of-battle tactics during the Second and Third Dutch Wars. A shortage of funding by the Restoration government resulted in the Dutch gaining the upper hand during the fighting of 1665–67, but when peace came the English fleet was expanded and larger and more powerful 'ships-of-the-line' were brought into service. These were vessels that were purpose-built to fight in line-of-battle formation. This, combined with superior English firepower, ensured the defeat of the Dutch in the final clash of 1672–74. By the end of these campaigns, the ship-of-the-line was fully evolved – a type of warship that would rule the seas until the advent of the steam-powered warship.

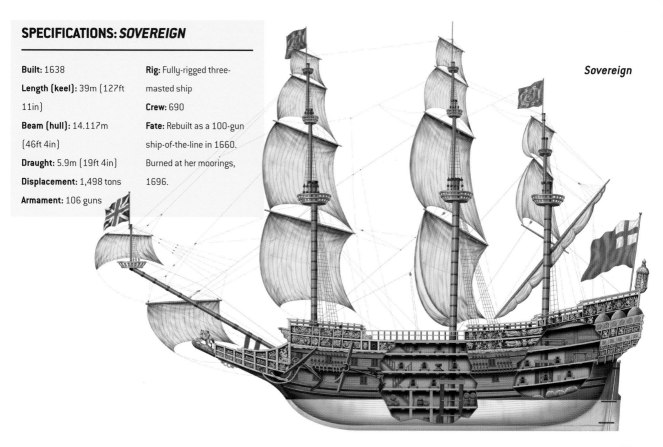

## SPECIFICATIONS: *SOVEREIGN*

**Built:** 1638

**Length (keel):** 39m (127ft 11in)

**Beam (hull):** 14.117m (46ft 4in)

**Draught:** 5.9m (19ft 4in)

**Displacement:** 1,498 tons

**Armament:** 106 guns

**Rig:** Fully-rigged three-masted ship

**Crew:** 690

**Fate:** Rebuilt as a 100-gun ship-of-the-line in 1660. Burned at her moorings, 1696.

*Sovereign*

**Brederode**

## Ship details

**Previous page:** One of the most remarkable ships of her age, the *Sovereign of the Seas* was built by Peter Pett for King Charles I and she was launched in 1637. She was the most expensive warship in the world, as well as the largest and most powerful. In 1651 she was renamed the *Sovereign*, and served as the flagship of the gifted Admiral Blake. The Dutch nicknamed her 'The Golden Devil'.

**This page:** As the largest warship in the Dutch fleet, the *Brederode* served as the flagship of both Admiral Tromp and Admiral de Ruyter during the First Dutch War. She carried 54 guns, was built in Rotterdam and first entered service in 1646. She survived several battles, including that of Scheveningen (1653) when Tromp was killed on board. She was finally lost in action against the Swedes in 1658.

# PIRATE SHIPS

The 'Golden Age of Piracy' is used as historical shorthand to cover the era during the late 17th and early 18th centuries when piracy was endemic, particularly in the waters of the Caribbean, the Atlantic seaboard of North America, the West African coast and the Indian Ocean. The real core of piratical activity was much shorter, lasting for a decade, starting around 1715. For the most part, pirates of this era used small single-masted sloops – which was probably the most common type of vessel in American waters during this period – as they possessed qualities that lent themselves to piracy. They were fast, which was useful when chasing a prize or evading a warship; they were shallow-draughted, so they could operate in shallow coastal waters where larger vessels couldn't go; and they could be sailed by less than a dozen crewmen.

Almost as popular was the brigantine, which was slightly larger, and therefore could carry more guns. Most pirate crews augmented their armament by guns taken from prizes, cutting extra gunports in their vessel's bulwarks when required. The more successful pirates – ones like Blackbeard, Sam Bellamy or Bartholomew Roberts – 'traded up' by replacing their smaller pirate vessels with larger prizes. Of these, the most popular larger vessel was the slave ship, as they were designed for speed as well as capacity.

Once they captured a ship, pirate crews would usually modify it to suit their needs. Superfluous superstructure such as large forecastles and sterncastles were removed, partly to improve the vessel's sailing qualities but also to make it an open fighting platform. Cabins and internal divisions were also removed. Not only did this make the vessel easier to fight from, but it suited the egalitarian ethos of the pirates themselves. Additional guns would be carried, either mounted in place on the upper or first decks, or lowered into the hold as ballast. The only drawback of these large pirate ships was that they drew attention to themselves, and so made it harder for the pirates to evade death or capture.

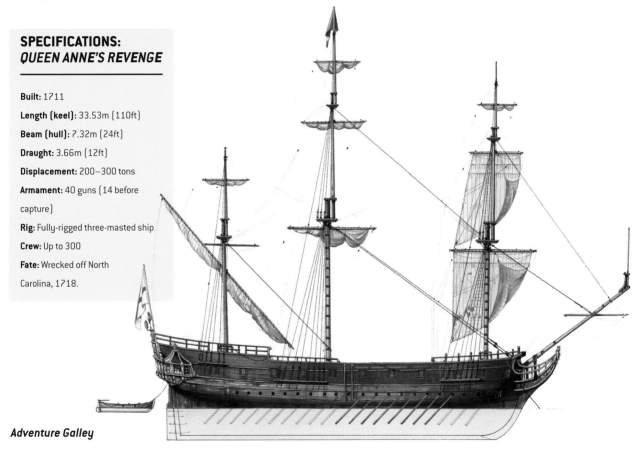

## SPECIFICATIONS:
### *QUEEN ANNE'S REVENGE*

**Built:** 1711

**Length (keel):** 33.53m (110ft)

**Beam (hull):** 7.32m (24ft)

**Draught:** 3.66m (12ft)

**Displacement:** 200–300 tons

**Armament:** 40 guns (14 before capture)

**Rig:** Fully-rigged three-masted ship

**Crew:** Up to 300

**Fate:** Wrecked off North Carolina, 1718.

*Adventure Galley*

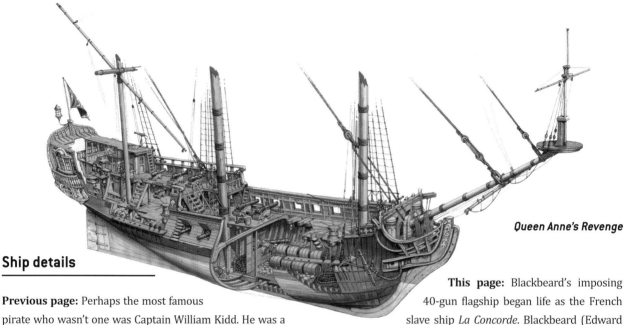

*Queen Anne's Revenge*

## Ship details

**Previous page:** Perhaps the most famous pirate who wasn't one was Captain William Kidd. He was a privateer who was given command of the newly built *Adventure Galley* in 1698, and after an unsuccessful cruise in the Indian Ocean he was hanged for crimes he didn't commit. As a 'galley' the *Adventure* could operate under both oar and sail. Her hull rotted quickly, and Kidd abandoned her in Madagascar before returning home.

**This page:** Blackbeard's imposing 40-gun flagship began life as the French slave ship *La Concorde*. Blackbeard (Edward Teach) captured her off Martinique in November 1718, and used her as his flagship during his blockade of Charles Town (Charleston) the following spring. Blackbeard then deliberately ran the *Queen Anne's Revenge* aground in Topsail Inlet (near modern-day Beaufort, North Carolina), as his large ship had become a liability. Instead he 'downsized' to a small sloop.

# WARSHIPS OF THE WAR OF INDEPENDENCE

**W**hen Britain's North American colonies rebelled in 1775, the Royal Navy was one of the strongest naval forces in the world. For their part, the American rebels had to build a fleet from scratch. The first American warships were actually privateers – privately owned vessels which were used to prey on British merchant ships. The American privateering fleet grew rapidly, and was soon augmented by small state-run warships. From these modest roots the modern US Navy was born.

In November 1775, the Continental Congress authorized the purchase of four merchant ships and a sloop, which were to be converted into warships. The largest of these – the *Alfred* and *Columbus* – displaced less than 280 tons, but what they lacked in size they made up for in speed. After all, this fledgling Continental Navy would be unable to match the British at sea, so the ability to outrun any pursuers was of primary importance. These were all-American-built ships, but Congress also purchased vessels abroad. For instance, the *Bonhomme Richard* was a French merchantman, converted into a warship by the French, and then presented to the Continental Congress.

The problem with all these vessels was that none of them were purpose-built warships. They were therefore not designed to carry a large complement of heavy guns, or built to withstand the pounding of enemy shot. Therefore, in December 1775, Congress approved the building of 13 frigates – one for each rebelling colony – armed with 24–32 guns apiece. Further warships were authorized from 1776 onwards, including three ships-of-the-line. Not all of these were completed – for instance only one ship-of-the-line was built, and she wasn't completed until the very end of hostilities.

Ultimately the US Navy played a relatively minor part in the struggle for independence. Britain's superiority at sea and her blockade of American ports rendered it almost impossible to conduct anything other than small-scale operations. However, by the end of the war two sloops-of-war, 16 frigates and one ship-of-the-line were built with Congressional approval.

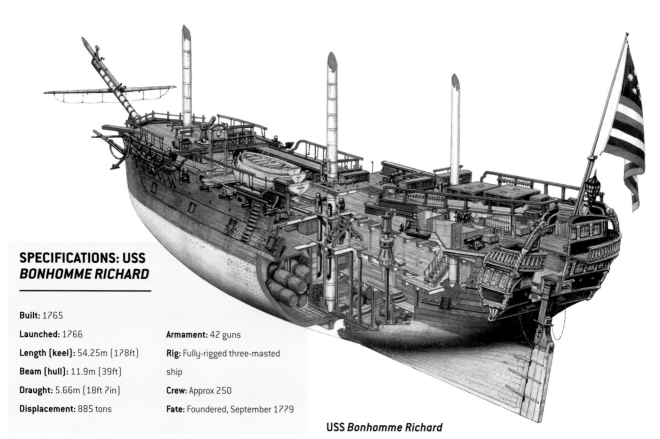

## SPECIFICATIONS: USS *BONHOMME RICHARD*

**Built:** 1765

**Launched:** 1766

**Length (keel):** 54.25m (178ft)

**Beam (hull):** 11.9m (39ft)

**Draught:** 5.66m (18ft 7in)

**Displacement:** 885 tons

**Armament:** 42 guns

**Rig:** Fully-rigged three-masted ship

**Crew:** Approx 250

**Fate:** Foundered, September 1779

**USS *Bonhomme Richard***

# Ship details

**Previous page:** Perhaps the most famous vessel of the War of Independence, the *Bonhomme Richard* began life as the French Indiaman *Duc de Duras*, launched in 1766. By 1779 she was old and worn, but in the hands of Captain John Paul Jones she enjoyed a brief but successful second career as an American warship, before sinking after Jones' victory over the British frigate *Serapis* off Flamborough Head in September 1779.

**This page:** One of the first frigates to enter service in the Continental Navy, the *Hancock* was built in Massachusetts and was launched in June 1776. After fitting out she left Boston the following July, and captured a British frigate before being pursued by a British squadron and then captured on 8 July. She was duly renamed HMS *Iris*, and remained in British service until her capture by the French in 1781.

**USS *Hancock***

# NAPOLEONIC SHIP-OF-THE-LINE

A century after the evolution of the ship-of-the-line in the mid-17th century, this 'battleship' of the age of sail had evolved into a highly practical and powerful weapon of war. Since their inception ships-of-the-line had been classed according to the number of guns they carried. By the 1760s a First Rate carried 100 guns or more, a Second Rate at least 80 and a Third Rate 64 or more guns. By the 1790s smaller Fourth and Fifth Rates were deemed not big enough to stand in the line of battle. These figures varied slightly over the decades, but the same international rating system remained in place throughout the 'Age of Fighting Sail'. With the exception of First Rates, all of these ships-of-the-line carried their guns on two continuous gun decks, not counting the few light pieces or carronades mounted on the exposed upper deck. First Rates boasted three gun decks – or four in the case of the imposing Spanish ship-of-the-line *Santisima Trinidad*.

At the start of the French Revolutionary War in 1793, the Royal Navy had 143 ships-of-the-line, although many of these were 'in ordinary' (mothballed), and needed several months of work before they could join the fleet. By 1801 this total had risen to 180, although many of the older ships-of-the-line were subsequently retired from service.

Not only did the fleet continue to grow during the remainder of the Napoleonic Wars, but by its close in 1815 the way ships were built had also changed. A shortage of suitable timber led to the use of iron fittings, which provided greater strength than the old wooden frames and beams, and therefore allowed the deployment of heavier guns. This move to increase the fighting potential of ships-of-the-line remained a noticeable feature throughout the Napoleonic period. Firepower was also increased by the introduction of carronades during the 1780s, which greatly increased the short-range firepower of warships. However, the real key to British success during the period was the professionalism, both of the crew and of the men who led these formidable vessels into action.

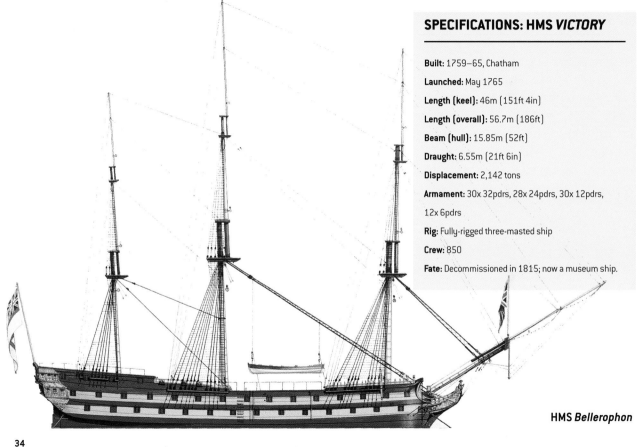

**Built:** 1759–65, Chatham

**Launched:** May 1765

**Length (keel):** 46m (151ft 4in)

**Length (overall):** 56.7m (186ft)

**Beam (hull):** 15.85m (52ft)

**Draught:** 6.55m (21ft 6in)

**Displacement:** 2,142 tons

**Armament:** 30x 32pdrs, 28x 24pdrs, 30x 12pdrs, 12x 6pdrs

**Rig:** Fully-rigged three-masted ship

**Crew:** 850

**Fate:** Decommissioned in 1815; now a museum ship.

**HMS *Bellerophon***

## Ship details

**Previous page:** The backbone of the British battle fleet was the 74-gun Third Rate ship-of-the-line, exemplified here by *Bellerophon*. Launched in 1786, she proved an excellent design, combining good sailing qualities with a powerful armament. Although later 74s were larger, *Bellerophon* and other 'Common 74s' were better all-round warships. She fought in three major actions – the Battle of the First of June, the Nile and Trafalgar – and was finally decommissioned in 1815.

**This page:** Undoubtedly the most famous warship of the 'Age of Fighting Sail', *Victory* was first laid down in Chatham in 1759, and completed six years later. She was the only First Rate designed by Sir Thomas Slade, and reputedly proved as fast and manoeuvrable as a Third Rate. She served in five major actions, but she is best remembered as the flagship of Vice-Admiral Nelson at the battle of Trafalgar (1805).

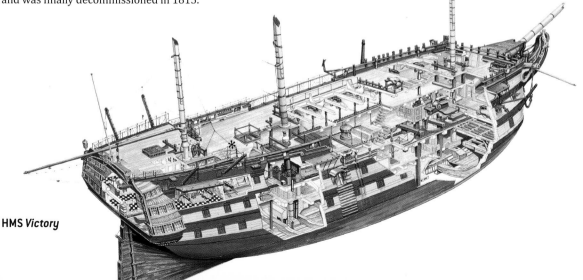

**HMS *Victory***

# IRONCLADS

The mid-19th century saw a major transformation in the way warships were built and functioned. The development of reliable steam-powered marine propulsion during the early 19th century created a viable alternative to wind power and by the mid-19th century, the majority of warships were steam-powered, and propulsive force was achieved using screw propellers or paddlewheels. Paddlewheels were vulnerable to enemy fire, but were better suited for use in craft operating in shallow coastal waters or rivers. At the same time, the advent of the shell gun rendered wooden-hulled warships obsolete, as they could be destroyed with relative ease. The solution was to protect warships with iron. The first true 'ironclad' was the French warship *La Gloire*, built in 1859. The British countered this by launching the even more powerful ironclad HMS *Warrior* in 1860. These ironclads dramatically altered naval warfare, as they were virtually invulnerable to enemy fire.

During the American Civil War (1861–65) the Confederacy had limited resources, so it was decided to maximize what little they had by converting existing ships into ironclads. The steam frigate USS *Merrimac* had been burned to the waterline in Norfolk, Virginia, and the Confederates rebuilt her as the ironclad CSS *Virginia* – a powerful but ungainly version of *Warrior* and *La Gloire*. This type of vessel became known as the casemate ironclad, as all its guns were protected by an iron casemate – an ironclad box-like superstructure that sat on top of the largely submerged hull.

Throughout the conflict, the Confederates built several ironclads of varying degrees of size and effectiveness, while the Union concentrated on the building of monitors. However, on the Mississippi River and its tributaries, the Union built a flotilla of casemate ironclads to help wrest control of the river from the Confederates. These were effectively lightly armoured but well-armed versions of paddlewheel steamers. Although they were completely unsuited to service on the open sea, their shallow draught made them ideal for riverine operations.

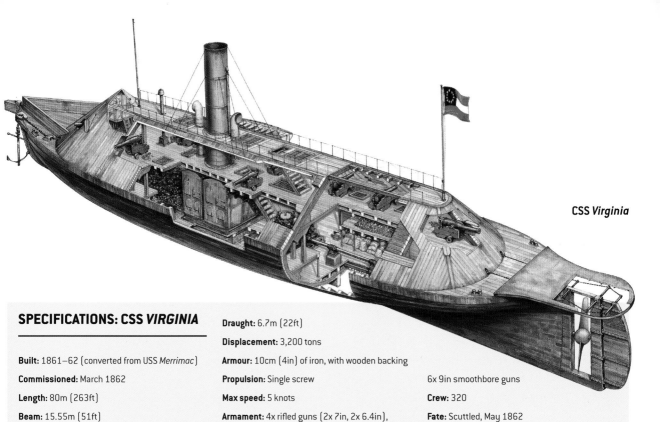

CSS *Virginia*

## SPECIFICATIONS: CSS *VIRGINIA*

**Built:** 1861–62 (converted from USS *Merrimac*)

**Commissioned:** March 1862

**Length:** 80m (263ft)

**Beam:** 15.55m (51ft)

**Draught:** 6.7m (22ft)

**Displacement:** 3,200 tons

**Armour:** 10cm (4in) of iron, with wooden backing

**Propulsion:** Single screw

**Max speed:** 5 knots

**Armament:** 4x rifled guns (2x 7in, 2x 6.4in),

6x 9in smoothbore guns

**Crew:** 320

**Fate:** Scuttled, May 1862

## Ship details

**Previous page:** The CSS *Virginia* was built using the lower hull and overhauled machinery of the wooden steam frigate USS *Merrimac*, augmented by a barn-like wooden casemate protected by iron plate. This revolutionary design rendered the vessel slow and difficult to manoeuvre, but it also rendered her impervious to enemy fire. She is best remembered for her duel with the USS *Monitor* in March 1862.

**This page:** One of seven City Class casemate river ironclads, *Cairo* was built in Mound City, Illinois, during late 1861 and entered service in January 1862. Despite her ungainly appearance she was an effective warship, although her light armour proved more vulnerable than expected. Her armoured casemate protected her large centreline paddlewheel as well as her main gun battery. She saw extensive service, but sank after striking a mine in December 1862.

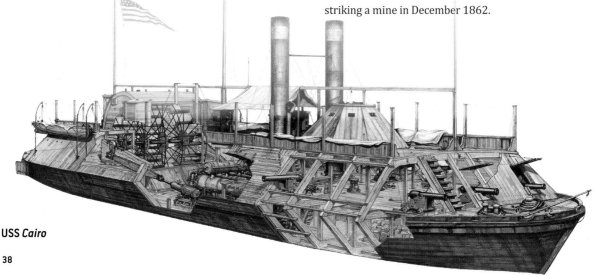

**USS *Cairo***

# UNION MONITORS

When reports of the building of the CSS *Virginia* reached Washington, money was set aside to produce a Union ironclad to counter her. In September 1861 contracts were awarded to three designers, one of whom was the Swedish-born inventor John Ericsson. Two of the designs for ironclads were relatively conventional. One was for a gunboat which became the USS *Galena*, and another for an American version of *La Gloire*, which was eventually christened the USS *New Ironsides*. By contrast Ericsson's design was completely revolutionary.

His plans centred around a revolving iron turret 6m (20ft) in diameter which contained two heavy guns. It was formed from curved sheets of iron 2.5cm (1in) thick which were layered together to form a protective wall 20cm (8in) thick. It was mounted on top of an iron hull which sat very low in the water, helping protect it from enemy shot. It was built in two parts – an armoured upper section and a more conventional unprotected lower hull. Steam was used to power the turret, and gave this strange vessel its propulsive power. The vessel was dubbed the USS *Monitor*, and it entered service in early February 1862. The USS *Monitor* fought her famous duel with the CSS *Virginia* on 9 March, and while the four-hour battle was indecisive, the *Monitor* fulfilled her mission – the protection of the wooden-hulled Union blockading squadron. Ericsson's design was dubbed a great success, and soon 'monitor fever' swept the North as the press clamoured for more ironclads based on Ericsson's design.

Although the *Monitor* herself foundered off Cape Hatteras in December, by then three other monitors of the Passaic Class had entered service, and more were on their way. By the end of the war in April 1865 over two dozen monitors had been built, and had proved their worth on the rivers and off the ports of the Confederacy as the Union stranglehold on the South grew tighter. These later ironclads were improved versions of the original *Monitor*, and some even boasted two turrets.

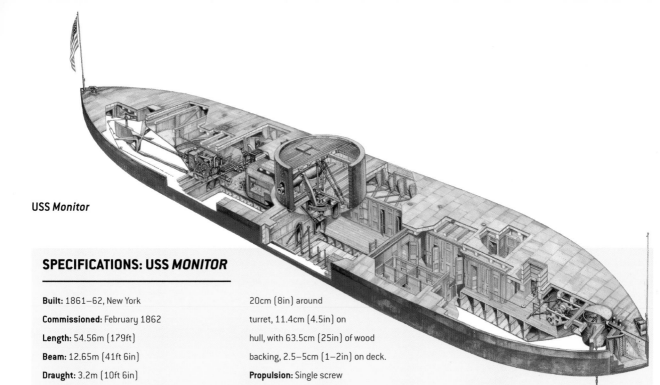

USS *Monitor*

## SPECIFICATIONS: USS *MONITOR*

**Built:** 1861–62, New York

**Commissioned:** February 1862

**Length:** 54.56m (179ft)

**Beam:** 12.65m (41ft 6in)

**Draught:** 3.2m (10ft 6in)

**Displacement:** 3,200 tons

**Armour:** 23cm (9in) of iron around pilot house,

20cm (8in) around turret, 11.4cm (4.5in) on hull, with 63.5cm (25in) of wood backing, 2.5–5cm (1–2in) on deck.

**Propulsion:** Single screw

**Max speed:** 6–9 knots

**Armament:** 2x 11in smoothbores

**Crew:** 49

**Fate:** Foundered, December 1862

# Ship details

**Previous page:** Although sceptics dubbed the *Monitor* 'a cheesebox on a raft', John Ericsson's design was the perfect counter to the *Virginia*. She was considerably smaller, and so low in the water that she was hard to hit. She was also much more manoeuvrable, and while the Confederate ironclad had to keep turning to bring her guns to bear, the *Monitor*'s guns could fire at the enemy regardless of the ironclad's heading.

**This page:** Following the *Monitor*'s success, ten similar 'monitors' were ordered, although their design would incorporate several improvements to the original vessel, following the suggestions of *Monitor*'s officers. The most significant of these was the mounting of the pilot house above the turret, ensuring the captain, helmsman and gunners remained in constant communication with each other during a battle.

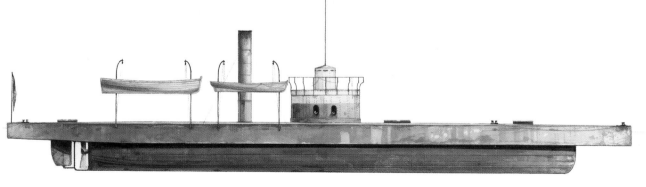

**USS *Weehawken***

# RIVER GUNBOATS

During the American Civil War, the Mississippi River was of vital strategic importance. Along with its northern tributaries, it flowed through states loyal to the Union and then ran south through the heartland of the Confederacy. The South's economy largely depended on the export of cotton and the Mississippi was the leading artery for its export. The Confederates protected their river and its major tributaries by constructing a series of forts and by building a small fleet of wooden gunboats. Dubbed the River Defense Fleet, this assortment of frail wooden vessels was poorly armed, but most were fitted with rams at their bow, which dictated the tactics these craft would use. To counter them the Union also built a fleet of gunboats, some of which were fitted with rams. This force, the Mississippi River Squadron, was supported by a growing number of Union river ironclads, such as the USS *Cairo* and her sisters.

For the most part these frail little warships were unarmoured. Some Union craft were protected by sheets of tin, while the Confederates employed bales of cotton to soak up enemy shot. While the Confederacy lacked the shipbuilding facilities to build fleets of custom-built warships, they made good use of the limited resources they had. This meant converting existing river steamers into makeshift warships, and protecting them as best they could using the cotton that could no longer be exported, thanks to the Union blockade of Southern ports.

During the campaign for the Mississippi River these fleets of small gunboats performed well, supporting army operations, engaging shore defences, running past enemy forts, escorting troop transports, scouting for the enemy and fighting desperate battles for control of the great river. The most significant of these engagements was the battle of Memphis, fought just above the city on 6 June 1862. The Confederate River Defense Fleet was annihilated by a powerful squadron of five casemate ironclads. For the remainder of the war the Union gunboats had no serious opposition, save Confederate torpedoes (mines) and shore defences.

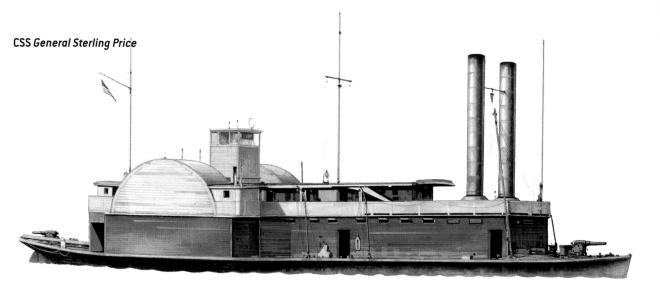

CSS *General Sterling Price*

## SPECIFICATIONS: USS *QUEEN OF THE WEST*

**Built:** 1854, Cincinnati, Illinois

**Purchased by Confederates:** May 1862

**Length:** 54.9m (180ft)

**Beam:** 11.4m (37ft 6in)

**Draught:** Approx 1.2m (4ft)

**Displacement:** 406 tons

**Propulsion:** Steam engine, twin side paddlewheels

**Max speed:** Approx 9 knots

**Armour:** None

**Armament:** 1x 30pdr smoothbore, 2x 12pdr howitzers

**Crew:** 120

**Fate:** Captured by Confederacy, June 1862; sunk, April 1863.

## Ship details

**Previous page:** This small wooden gunboat was typical of the vessels of the Confederate River Defense Fleet. Previously a civilian riverboat, in 1862 she was converted by adding a ram bow and additional protection to her hull and superstructure. She was sunk at the battle of Memphis, but was later raised and ended the war as a Union gunboat.

**This page:** In 1862 this civilian paddlewheel riverboat was purchased by the Union and converted into a lightly armed ram, one of several developed by Colonel Charles Ellet during the war. She took part in the battle of Memphis and in attacks on Vicksburg, but ended the war serving the Confederates. She carries a tin-plate letter 'Q' between her smokestacks as an identifying mark.

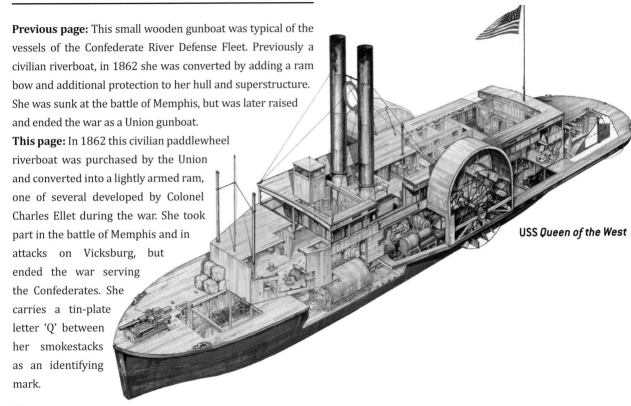

USS *Queen of the West*

# COMMERCE RAIDERS

**A**lthough the Confederacy lacked the ships, men and resources of the Union during the American Civil War, they became very adept at using what they had to defend their coasts and harbours. This though, was a purely passive style of naval warfare – the aim being to defend the Confederacy. In order to actually inflict damage to the Union cause the Confederate Navy needed to find a way to take the war to the enemy. The solution was the development of the commerce raider.

The aim of these vessels was to destroy enemy merchant shipping, which would harm the enemy financially and put pressure on politicians to bring the war to an end. This was a tactic that had been used since the medieval period, as privateers – private men of war – harried enemy shipping. American privateers had been employed during the American War of Independence and the War of 1812, so it was a device that was well understood by the Confederate naval strategists. This time, though, these commerce raiders would be owned and operated by the Confederate Navy, rather than by individual privateers.

Commerce raiders needed to be sturdy, self-sufficient and fast, however, for the most part the Confederates lacked ships that were suitable for conversion into commerce raiders. The solution was to buy or build them overseas. An exception was the CSS *Sumter*, which was converted from a Philadelphia-registered steamer impounded in New Orleans. Under the command of Captain Ralph Semmes it slipped out past the Union blockade in June 1861 and captured 18 ships within six months. After being trapped in Gibraltar by Union blockaders she was sold and her crew returned home. Other notable commerce raiders were the CSS *Florida*, CSS *Alabama* and CSS *Shenandoah*, all of which were built in British ports. The *Florida* captured 37 prizes before her capture in October 1864, while the *Alabama* – the most famous of the commerce raiders – captured 65 Union vessels during a cruise that lasted almost two years. She was eventually sunk off Cherbourg in June 1864.

## SPECIFICATIONS: CSS *ALABAMA*

**Built:** Birkenhead

**Launched:** May 1862

**Length:** 67m (220ft)

**Beam:** 9.68m (31ft 9in)

**Draught:** 4.27m (14ft)

**Displacement:** 1,050 tons

**Propulsion:** Single screw-propulsion

**Max speed:** 13 knots

**Armament:** 1x 110pdr rifle, 1x 68pdr smoothbore, 6x 32pdr smoothbores

**Crew:** 138

**Fate:** Sunk, 19 June 1864

CSS *Alabama*

# Ship details

**Previous page:** The *Alabama* was a purpose-built commerce raider, built amid great secrecy in Birkenhead. She put to sea in August 1862, and her new commander Ralph Semmes began a cruise that would ultimately last for nearly two years, and involve her ranging as far afield as the coast of South America and the Indian Ocean. This elegant vessel was the most successful commerce raider of the war.

**This page:** In September 1864 the Confederacy purchased a steamer in Glasgow, and had her converted into the commerce raider CSS *Shenandoah*. She began her cruise the following month, and spent a year at sea, circumnavigating the globe and capturing 38 prizes, many of them Union whaling ships. She was still at large when the war ended, and she finally surrendered to the British authorities in Liverpool in November 1865.

# BRITISH DREADNOUGHTS

**M**uch as the creation of the first ironclad had done almost half a century earlier, the launch of HMS *Dreadnought* in February 1906 transformed naval warfare. Previously, battleships were well enough armoured, but for the most part they were armed with just four main guns, in two twin turrets. Secondary armament was designed to augment this main firepower, while tertiary batteries protected the ship from attack by smaller vessels. This meant that in action guns of various calibres would engage the enemy at the same time, creating no end of problems for the gunnery directors. *Dreadnought* changed all that.

She was armed with ten 12in guns, mounted in five turrets. They were spaced around the ship so four turrets could fire to either side, unleashing a broadside twice as powerful as those produced by 'pre-dreadnought' battleships. She was powered by steam turbines, which made her faster than all contemporary battleships, while her hull and turrets were extremely well protected by armour.

The result was a warship which rendered all existing battleships obsolete. At first the British Admiralty were reluctant to embrace this radical design of warship, but the threat of foreign naval powers pre-empting them led to them being swayed by the First Sea Lord, Sir John 'Jackie' Fisher. Designed by Sir Philip White, *Dreadnought* was built in record time and she was commissioned in December 1906. As all previous battleships were now obsolete, Germany seized this opportunity to gain parity with Britain. So began a naval arms race that saw whole fleets of 'dreadnoughts' being built. Britain laid down the first of these new capital ships in late 1906, and within five years there were ten dreadnoughts in service. These were built in batches of three ships or fewer, which allowed minor improvements to be made with each new design, and experimentation with the turret configuration to allow all main guns to fire in a single broadside. By 1911, though, the decision was taken to increase the size of the main gun armament to 13.5in, which ushered in a new era in dreadnought design.

## SPECIFICATIONS: HMS *DREADNOUGHT*

**Built:** 1905–06, Portsmouth

**Length:** 160.63m (527ft)

**Beam:** 25m (82ft)

**Draught:** 9.45m (31ft)

**Displacement:** 21,845 tons (fully laden)

**Propulsion:** Four steam turbines and 18 boilers, generating 23,000shp

**Max speed:** 21 knots

**Armour:** 4–11in belt, 11in on turrets, barbettes and conning tower, 1.5–3in on deck

**Armament:** 10x 12in guns in 5 twin turrets, 24x 12pdr guns, 5x submerged 18in torpedo tubes

**Crew:** 695–773

**Fate:** Scrapped, 1921

HMS *Dreadnought*

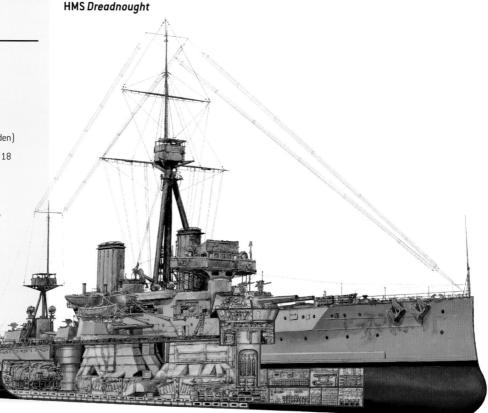

## Ship details

**Previous page:** The idea behind *Dreadnought* was the creation of 'the big gun battleship' – one which had a powerful main armament of heavy guns, all of the same calibre. This, combined with turbine propulsion and modern fire-control systems, made *Dreadnought* the most powerful warship of her day. Ironically, the world's first 'dreadnought' missed the great test of the battle of Jutland (1916), as *Dreadnought* was detached from the Grand Fleet at the time.

**This page:** The greatest drawback of the original *Dreadnought* design was that not all of her turrets could combine their fire into a single broadside, as two were mounted abreast of each other amidships. Various design solutions were considered, including the superimposing of one turret above and behind another. This was first done in *Neptune*. Her midships guns were also staggered, to give them a restricted ability to fire to either beam.

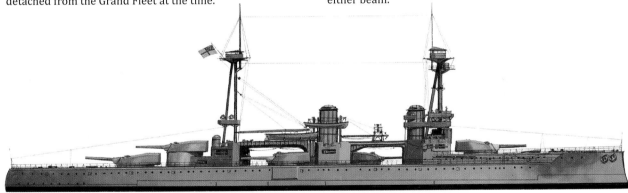

**HMS *Neptune***

# GERMAN DREADNOUGHTS

The launch of the *Dreadnought* in early 1906 came as a shock to the German Navy. However, this development also represented an opportunity, as Britain and Germany would both have to rebuild their battle fleets from scratch and so would be on an equal footing. So, considerable resources were expended on the creation of a German dreadnought fleet – one that would one day be able to challenge British naval supremacy. Naval designers were ordered to abandon plans to build more pre-dreadnought battleships, and instead a German dreadnought was designed: the first of these was laid down in the summer of 1907. These Nassau Class vessels were the first German dreadnoughts. While similar in concept to *Dreadnought*, these German dreadnoughts were no slavish copies. Instead their design emphasized different priorities. They carried 12 11in guns, mounted in six twin turrets. However, due to their configuration only eight guns could fire in any one broadside. They were also slower than *Dreadnought*, but were better protected.

By the time the fourth German dreadnought was launched in late 1908, the Anglo-German naval arms race was in full swing. By then a new group of four Helgoland Class dreadnoughts had been laid down, which were due to enter service by late 1911. They were similar to the Nassau Class, featuring the same rather wasteful 'hexagonal' arrangement of six twin turrets; German naval architects were still deciding how best to arrange a dreadnought's heavy guns, and the need for speedy construction outweighed considerations of perfection. The solution was to stagger the centre turrets slightly. So, in the next batch of four Kaiser Class dreadnoughts, with ten 12in guns in five turrets, one of the after turrets was superimposed over the other. The midship guns were also staggered, to offer a limited angle of fire across the deck. The problem was properly solved in the König Class which followed. These carried 12in guns in five turrets, deployed along the centreline, and they formed the core of Germany's High Seas Fleet at the battle of Jutland (1916).

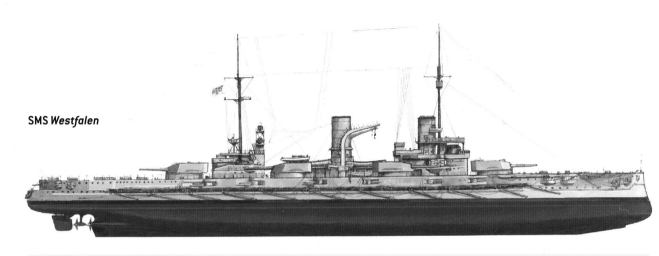

SMS *Westfalen*

## SPECIFICATIONS: SMS *FRIEDRICH DER GROSSE*

**Built:** 1910–12, Hamburg

**Length:** 172.5m (566ft)

**Beam:** 29m (95ft)

**Draught:** 9.14m (30ft)

**Displacement:** 27,000 tons (fully laden)

**Propulsion:** Three steam turbines, generating 31,000shp

**Max speed:** 23½ knots

**Armour:** 4–14in belt, 12in on turrets, 16in on conning tower, 1.5in on deck

**Armament:** 10x 12in guns in 5 twin turrets, 14x 5.9in guns, 12x 3.5in guns, 5x submerged 20in torpedo tubes

**Crew:** 1,178

**Fate:** Scuttled, 1919

# Ship details

**Previous page:** Commissioned in November 1909, the *Westfalen* was the second German dreadnought to enter service. Her 12 11in guns were arranged in a 'hexagonal' configuration, which was seen as wasteful as only eight guns could fire on each broadside. Despite wasting a third of her guns, she was still considerably more powerful than earlier German pre-dreadnoughts, and was considered the equal of the original British *Dreadnought*.

**This page:** This Kaiser Class warship represented the third generation of German dreadnoughts, and boasted a heavier gun calibre, a better turret configuration and greatly improved armoured protection than its predecessors. Her 12in guns were laid out so that ten guns could fire on each broadside. During the battle of Jutland, *Friedrich der Grosse* served as the flagship of the commander of the High Seas Fleet, Vice-Admiral Scheer.

**SMS *Friedrich der Grosse***

# SUPER DREADNOUGHTS

The difference between a 'dreadnought' and a 'super dreadnought' was the calibre of her main armament. All British dreadnoughts carried 12in guns, while their German counterparts carried 11in and 12in ordnance. In the late summer of 1908 the British Admiralty learned that the Germans were designing larger calibre guns and therefore the decision was made to increase the size of British dreadnought ordnance to 13.5in. These guns were too large and heavy to be incorporated in any existing style of dreadnought, so naval architects were forced to come up with a fresh approach. Their solution was embodied in the first group of super dreadnoughts to enter service – the four vessels of the Orion Class. These guns were too heavy to permit them to be off-centred amidships, as in earlier dreadnoughts, so instead they were mounted along the centreline of the vessel. 'B' and 'X' turrets were superimposed, so they could fire over the top of 'A' and 'Y' turrets. A fifth turret was mounted amidships. The design proved successful, and the ships entered service in 1912. By then a second batch of super dreadnoughts were being built. These four King George V Class were soon followed by four slightly improved versions, which formed the Iron Duke Class.

In the end, the Germans never perfected their new heavy ordnance until after the Kaiser and König classes were built. However, more reports that they had developed a 15in gun prompted the British to build their own 15in gun super dreadnoughts. In fact, thanks to their excellent propulsive systems these five Queen Elizabeth Class vessels were dubbed 'fast battleships'. They carried four 15in guns in four turrets, two forward, two aft. The same configuration was repeated in the Royal Sovereign Class. These fast battleships were probably the finest capital ships of the war. In late 1913 the Germans laid down the first of their own Bayern Class super dreadnoughts. Like the Queen Elizabeths they carried eight 15in guns in four centreline turrets, but only two of these powerful modern battleships were commissioned.

## SPECIFICATIONS: HMS *IRON DUKE*

**Built:** 1912–14, Portsmouth

**Length:** 190m (622ft 9in)

**Beam:** 27.43m (90ft)

**Draught:** 9m (29ft 6in)

**Displacement:** 29,560 tons (fully laden)

**Propulsion:** Steam turbines, generating 29,000shp

**Max speed:** 21¼ knots

**Armour:** 4–12in belt, 11in on turrets and conning
tower, 1–2.5in on deck

**Armament:** 10x 13.5in guns in 5 twin turrets, 12x 6in
guns, 2x 3in guns, 5x submerged 21in torpedo tubes

**Crew:** 718

**Fate:** Scrapped, 1946

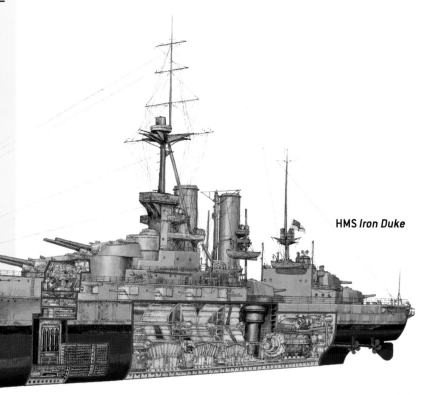

HMS *Iron Duke*

## Ship details

**Previous page:** The *Iron Duke* and her three sister ships represented the final development of the British super dreadnought. Although the fast battleships that followed were considered super dreadnoughts, their speed put them in a class of their own. The Iron Duke Class were powerful warships, whose design embraced considerable improvements over their predecessors. *Iron Duke* served as the flagship of the Grand Fleet's commander Admiral Jellicoe during the battle of Jutland.

**This page:** The last battleships to be completed for the Imperial German Navy, these represented a belated attempt not just to equal the power of the latest British super dreadnoughts, but to surpass them in terms of firepower and quality of design. They were superb ships with four 12in guns, one of which was superimposed above and behind the other, and extremely thick armoured protection. The one exception was deck armour, which remained thin.

SMS *Bayern*

# AUSTRO-HUNGARIAN BATTLESHIPS

Austria-Hungary had no overseas empire, and didn't nurture ambitions to develop one. Its multi-cultural empire lay within its own borders, and it was the defence of these frontiers and control of the lands within them that dictated military policy. Originally its small navy was charged with defending its own coastline on the Adriatic Sea, but a boom in Austro-Hungarian mercantile shipping led to demands for a larger fleet. So, from 1890 onwards the Austro-Hungarian Navy embarked on a shipbuilding programme that would produce a small but well-balanced modern fleet. By 1900 the goal had evolved into the attainment of naval superiority in the Adriatic, and battleships were seen as the key to achieving this.

The three Monarch Class battleships of the 1890s were Austria-Hungary's first foray into modern battleships, but these were small coastal battleships rather than seagoing ones. Far more impressive were the three seagoing battleships of the Hapsburg Class. Their high speed, decent armour and 9.4in main guns made them useful additions to the fleet. However, they were still pre-dreadnoughts, as were the next batch of three Erzherzog Karl Class battleships, built between 1902 and 1907. The last two of these were still being completed when HMS *Dreadnought* entered service, thereby rendering them obsolete before they had even been commissioned.

The Austro-Hungarians scrapped all plans for more pre-dreadnoughts, and instead developed plans for dreadnoughts of their own. The first of these was a compromise, a type known as 'semi-dreadnoughts'. These Radetsky Class ships were first designed in 1905, but modifications meant that the first two were only laid down in 1907. A third semi-dreadnought would follow, and all three entered service in 1910–11. The first true Austro-Hungarian dreadnoughts were the four vessels of the Tegetthoff Class, which were unusual in that they carried their 12 12in guns in four triple turrets. Two of them were sunk during World War I, and the remaining two were given to the French and the Italian fleets at the end of the war.

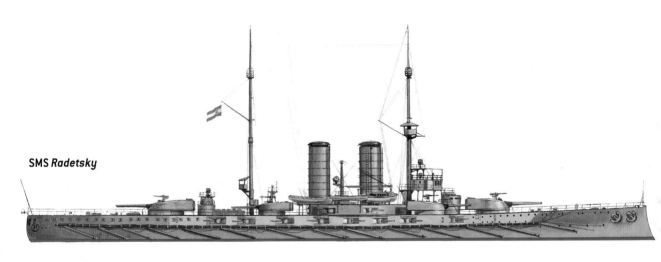

SMS *Radetsky*

## SPECIFICATIONS:
## SMS *VIRIBUS UNITIS*

**Built:** 1910–12, Trieste

**Length:** 152.17m (499ft 3in)

**Beam:** 27.33m (89ft 8in)

**Draught:** 8.84m (29ft)

**Displacement:** 21,600 tons (fully laden)

**Propulsion:** Steam turbines, generating 26,400shp

**Max speed:** 20 knots

**Armour:** 6–11in belt, 11in on turrets and conning

tower, 1¼–2in on deck

**Armament:** 12x 12in guns in 4 triple turrets, 12x 5.9in guns, 4x submerged 21in torpedo tubes

**Crew:** 1,087

**Fate:** Sunk, 1918

## Ship details

**Previous page:** The Austro-Hungarian naval designer Siegfried Popper had already developed plans for these vessels when *Dreadnought* was launched. He altered them to create a true dreadnought, but this design was rejected, as it was deemed too expensive. Instead Popper reconfigured this new class as semi-dreadnoughts, whose main armament consisted of guns of two different calibres – four 11in and eight 9.2in guns in six twin turrets. It was a cost-effective compromise.

**This page:** Austria-Hungary was finally spurred into commissioning her own dreadnoughts following the building of two by the Italians, who were seen as Austria-Hungary's principal naval threat. Their radical design involved four 12in turrets fore and aft, with the after turrets superimposed above the forward ones. Even more unusually each turret carried three guns. Three of these four powerful Tegetthoff Class dreadnoughts entered service before the outbreak of World War I.

**SMS *Viribus Unitis***

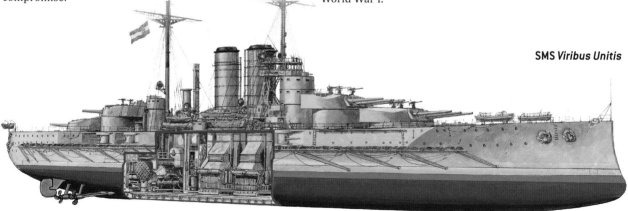

# BATTLECRUISERS

The revolution in naval thinking created by the building of *Dreadnought* led to some wrong turns in warship design. One of these was the development of the 'battlecruiser'. In the late 19th century the 'armoured cruiser' had been developed to destroy smaller and less powerful enemy cruisers on the high seas. It was therefore just a small step to imagine the effectiveness of a dreadnought-style equivalent. The British First Sea Lord, Sir 'Jackie' Fisher, was a staunch advocate of this idea, and came up with a new type of vessel. It would have the armament of a conventional dreadnought, but the speed of a cruiser. The balance between speed, armament and protection was something that required balance – an over-emphasis on one element usually meant a corresponding reduction in another. Fisher was happy to sacrifice armour in exchange for a greater emphasis on firepower and speed. The result was the 'battlecruiser'.

The first group of three battlecruisers were laid down in early 1906 and entered service in 1909. These Invincible Class battlecruisers were capable of steaming at 25 knots – roughly 4 knots faster than a dreadnought – and they carried a powerful armament of eight 12in guns. Their armour, though, had a maximum belt thickness of just 6in. Another group of three similar Indefatigable Class battleships followed soon afterwards, but already the design requirements had changed. The Admiralty now expected battlecruisers to carry 13.5in guns, and so the three Lion Class battlecruisers and the one-of-a-kind *Tiger* were developed to fulfil this need.

In Germany these developments were mirrored by the launch of an experimental battlecruiser *Von Der Tann* in 1909, a vessel that was soon followed by six more German battlecruisers, the last of which carried 12in guns. Unlike their British counterparts, the German battlecruisers were well protected – a factor that saved most of the German battlecruiser fleet at Jutland. Ultimately though, battlecruisers were a failure as they proved too vulnerable to be used in a fleet action – and were too powerful to be left out of one.

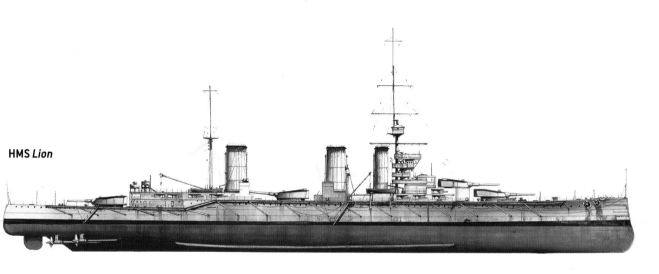

HMS *Lion*

## SPECIFICATIONS: HMS *LION*

**Built:** 1910–12, Devonport

**Length:** 201.17m (660ft)

**Beam:** 27m (88ft 5in)

**Draught:** 8m (26ft 6in)

**Displacement:** 26,350 tons (fully laden)

**Propulsion:** Steam turbines, generating 27,000shp

**Max speed:** 27 knots

**Armour:** 4–6in belt, 9–10in on turrets and conning tower, 1in on deck

**Armament:** 8x 13.5in guns in 4 triple turrets, 16x 4in guns, 2x submerged 21in torpedo tubes

**Crew:** 997

**Fate:** Scrapped, 1924

## Ship details

**Previous page:** The three Lion Class battlecruisers (*Lion*, *Queen Mary* and *Princess Royal*) were armed with 13.5in guns, and therefore represented a significant improvement in the firepower of British dreadnoughts. They were also larger and faster than their predecessors, and slightly better protected. *Lion* served as Vice-Admiral Beatty's flagship at Jutland and survived the battle, despite being hit 13 times. One of these hits destroyed 'Q' turret amidships, and almost destroyed her.

**This page:** *Lützow* represented an improvement in the fighting potential of the German battlecruiser fleet. She and her sisters *Derfflinger* and *Hindenburg* were well protected, both by armour and by watertight sub divisions. At Jutland *Lützow* flew the flag of Vice-Admiral Hipper, who commanded the German scouting forces. She was badly damaged during the battle, being hit 24 times, and despite her crew's best efforts she sank the day after the battle.

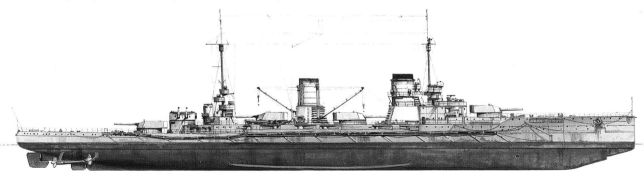

SMS *Lützow*

# DESTROYERS

The development of the self-propelled torpedo in 1868 ushered in a new threat to warships – attack by small torpedo-armed craft. This was a David versus Goliath struggle where the advantage often lay with the smaller vessel. During the late 19th century, torpedoes became ever more reliable and deadly. Range, speed and the size of the warhead all increased, making the torpedo a weapon that could no longer be ignored. Experiments were made into how best to launch these new-fangled torpedoes, and in 1876 the British produced a small 'torpedo boat' designed to fire its torpedo from a torpedo tube mounted on its forecastle. Developments by other European powers included boats where the torpedo was dropped over the stern, rolled off the side of the craft or fired from tubes mounted in the bows. By the late 1890s the French possessed the most advanced torpedo boats of the period, capable of launching two torpedoes simultaneously. These frail craft were the forerunners of the torpedo boats and destroyers of World War I.

The British countered this threat by building small craft of their own – small, fast vessels armed with little guns. These were designed to intercept and destroy torpedo boats, and so were dubbed 'torpedo boat destroyers', soon shortened to 'destroyer'. Strangely, most were armed with torpedoes of their own, so they could serve a dual purpose. By 1900 Britain had begun to build even faster turbine-powered torpedo destroyers, but these experimental craft proved too small to operate in the North Sea. Consequently from 1901 onwards the British built larger and more seaworthy versions. Soon the line between the torpedo boat and the destroyer had become so blurred that the two were effectively the same thing. The Germans were slower to adopt the destroyer, but during World War I British and German destroyers and torpedo boats clashed at Jutland, by which time they had become an indispensable part of a battle fleet – destroyers had become both protectors and attackers in one small, fast and nimble package.

HMS *Hornet*

## SPECIFICATIONS: HMS *OPAL*

**Built:** 1916, Sunderland

**Length:** 82m (269ft)

**Beam:** 8.38m (27ft 6in)

**Draught:** 3.2m (10ft 6in)

**Displacement:** 1,059 tons (fully laden)

**Propulsion:** Steam turbines, generating 25,000shp

**Max speed:** 34 knots

**Armour:** None

**Armament:** 3x 4in guns, 3x quick-firing 2pdr 'pom-poms', 2x 21in torpedo tubes

**Crew:** 80

**Fate:** Wrecked in January 1918 off Orkney.

# Ship details

**Previous page:** Completed in 1893, *Hornet* and her sister *Havoc* were the Royal Navy's first torpedo boat destroyers (TBDs). These small coal-fuelled craft were extremely cramped and uncomfortable when at sea, but their powerful engines gave them a top speed of 27 knots, and their armament of a 12pdr, three 6pdrs and two torpedo tubes gave them a formidable punch. However, the experimental *Hornet* soon became obsolete, and was scrapped in 1909.

**This page:** This and the preceding L Class were the mainstay of Britain's destroyer flotillas after 1915, and these small craft played a prominent part in the battle of Jutland. Originally just six M Class destroyers were built in 1914, but this force was soon expanded. A total of 85 Admiralty M Class destroyers were built during the war, the vessel names beginning with M, N, O and P, including HMS *Opal*.

**Admiralty M Class Destroyer**

# SUBMARINES

n 1914 the senior officers of both the British and German admiralties were still contemptuous of submarines, which many saw as little more than a gimmick that wasted valuable naval resources. They were soon proved wrong, and by war's end it was clear that the submarine or U-boat was a naval weapon of great importance – one whose growth in importance was balanced by a corresponding diminution of the value of the dreadnought. Before World War I, submarines were still seen as experimental vessels. The American inventor John P. Holland built several experimental submarines from 1896 onwards while in France the designer Max Lebeuf developed the first truly modern submarine in the 1890s – a boat with a pressure hull and external ballast tanks that established the shape of things to come. The Royal Navy built its first Holland type submarine in 1901, and by 1906 it boasted a squadron of six boats. Soon a further 38 more advanced C Class boats were ordered. The Imperial German Navy built its first U-boat in 1905 and dramatically expanded its submersible fleet in the years immediately preceding the outbreak of war.

For the most part these submersibles all operated according to similar principles. The boat's vitals – its crew and machinery – were contained within the pressure hull, which was built to withstand pressures of up to 40 fathoms (73m; 240ft). The outer hull protected the pressure hull and contained the ballast tanks that controlled a boat's ascent and descent. The most successful submersibles of the war were the large German U-boats built after 1915 that ranged far out into the Atlantic in search of prey. They had a surface speed in excess of 16 knots, and a submerged speed of just less than half that. They were powered by diesel engines, with electric batteries supplying power under water. These boats were armed with six torpedo tubes, which could be reloaded. These large and deadly U-boats were a far cry from the early Holland submersibles, and demonstrated the awful potential of the submarine as a weapon of war.

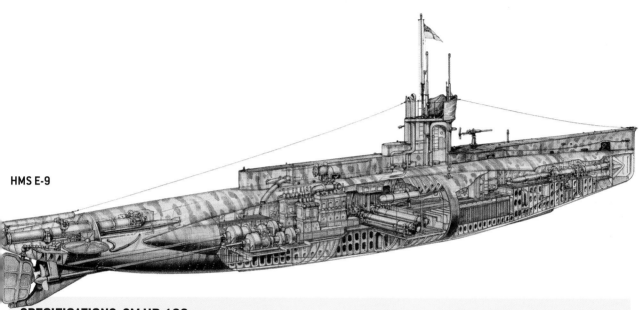

HMS E-9

## SPECIFICATIONS: SM UB-122

**Built:** 1917–18, Bremen

**Length:** 55.3m (181ft 5in)

**Beam:** 5.8m (19ft)

**Draught:** 3.7m (12ft)

**Displacement:** 516 tons (fully laden)

**Propulsion:** Steam turbines and electric batteries

**Max speed:** 13.6 knots (surfaced); 8 knots (submerged)

**Range:** 8,500 nautical miles

**Armament:** 5x torpedo tubes (4 forward, 1 aft), 10x 50cm torpedoes, 88mm deck gun

**Crew:** 34

**Fate:** Surrendered, November 1918

## Ship details

**Previous page:** The Royal Navy's E Class submarines represented a significant improvement over earlier British submersibles. These E Class boats had a number of unusual features, including not only bow and stern torpedo tubes, but transverse ones as well, fired from the control room. Under the command of Lieutenant Commander Horton, E-9 became the first British submarine to score a wartime kill when she sank the German cruiser *Hela* in September 1914.

**This page:** Of all the types of U-boat adopted by the Imperial German Navy during the war, UB-III was the most successful. It was a large late-war design and first entered service in 1917, in time for America's entry into the war. They were designed specifically for long-range cruising, and this allowed them to operate in the Atlantic sea lanes, where boats like this inflicted significant losses to Allied shipping.

**German UB-III Class U-boat**

# KRIEGSMARINE U-BOATS

The Treaty of Versailles expressly forbade Germany from rebuilding her U-boat fleet. However, by the 1920s German designers had begun to develop a new generation of U-boats, under the guise of building submersibles for export. These restrictions were lifted when the Nazis revoked the treaty in 1934. The following year Karl Dönitz became the commander of Germany's nascent U-boat fleet, and was largely left to devise a boatbuilding programme, training, strategy and tactics for his force. He envisaged the U-boat as primarily a torpedo boat which operated on the surface, and attacked at night, but could submerge when required to evade detection. This meant he favoured vessels that behaved well on the surface, with a long range and endurance.

In 1935–36 the first two experimental Type IA U-boats were laid down, as well as six Type IIA coastal submarines (designated U1 to U6). Subsequent versions of Type II U-boats were launched between 1935 and 1940, but by then these craft were designated as being too small for Dönitz's purposes. Instead, in 1934 he approved plans for a Type VII U-boat, and the first of these new ocean-going boats entered service in 1935–36. These were twice as large as their predecessors, and were fitted with one stern and four bow tubes, as well as a deck gun. This first batch of ten boats was dubbed Type VIIA, and they were soon followed by a larger and more powerful variant, which was designated VIIB. By the time war was declared in September 1939, there were 57 U-boats in service, and this number climbed steadily during 1940 and 1941.

In 1940 the first Type VIIC U-boats entered service – identical to the previous class, only slightly longer, and with an improved sonar – but these Type VII boats were the workhorses of the German U-boat fleet. Together they formed the wolfpacks which almost swung the tide of the war during the Battle of the Atlantic. In all, 24 type VIIB and 568 Type VIIC boats entered service. Only a handful of them survived the war.

Type VIIC

## SPECIFICATIONS: TYPE VIIC U-BOAT

**Built:** 1940–45

**Length:** 67.1m (220ft)

**Beam:** 6.2m (20ft 5in)

**Draught:** 4.8m (15ft 9in)

**Displacement:** 761 tons (surfaced), 865 tons (submerged)

**Speed:** 17 knots (surfaced), 7.6 knots (submerged)

**Endurance:** 6,500 nautical miles (surfaced), 80 nautical miles (submerged)

**Powerplant:** 2x 1,400bhp diesels coupled with 2x 375bhp electric motors

**Armament:** 5x torpedo tubes (4 bow, 1 stern), 1x 8.8cm gun, 1x 2cm gun

**Crew:** 44

**Type XXI**

## Ship details

**Previous page:** A Type VIIC U-boat, this vessel is typical of the majority of U-boats that saw service during the war. Vessels of this type were primarily deployed in the Atlantic, but they also saw service in the Mediterranean, the Indian Ocean and even the Pacific. However, their limited underwater endurance proved their downfall. As Allied anti-submarine capabilities increased, these boats became increasingly vulnerable and losses mounted steadily from late 1943 on.

**This page:** Towards the end of the war several new types of U-boat were developed under the guidance of Hellmuth Walter, resulting in the Type XXI class (or *Elektroboote*). These diesel-electric boats represented the next generation – craft designed to remain submerged for long periods, with a greatly improved underwater performance. Between 1943 and 1945 118 of them were built, but construction problems meant that only four ever became operational.

# GERMAN BATTLESHIPS

ollowing Adolf Hitler's rise to power in 1933, the Kriegsmarine was encouraged to develop a strategy based on a campaign fought in the Atlantic, so plans were drawn up for a small fleet of modern battleships and battlecruisers. The Treaty of Versailles limited German surface ships to 10,000 tons, and these terms were met – more or less – by the development of the *panzerschiffe* (armoured ship), known as the 'pocket battleship'. The first of these, the *Deutschland*, met the size requirements, but its two sister ships, *Admiral Scheer* and *Admiral Graf Spee*, commissioned in 1934–36, were slightly larger and displaced approximately 16,000 tons when fully laden. They carried a main armament of six 280mm (11in) guns mounted in two triple turrets. In 1939, *Deutschland* was renamed *Lützow*, to avoid the propaganda disaster of a ship called 'Germany' being sunk.

By 1935 Hitler had abandoned the restrictions of Versailles, and commissioned two large battlecruisers – *Scharnhorst* and *Gneisenau* – which entered service in 1938-39. With a fully laden displacement of 38,900 tons these warships were as well armoured as most battleships, but carried a relatively light armament of nine 280mm guns. Like the *panzerschiffe* they were designed primarily as commerce raiders, and were considered the German counter to the launch of the two French battleships of the Dunkerque Class. Far more ambitious were the two battleships of the Bismarck Class. *Bismarck* and *Tirpitz* were laid down in 1936 and entered service in 1940 and 1941 respectively. These were designed as a counter to British battleships and were every bit as powerful as the Nelson Class, despite having smaller calibre guns. With a displacement of over 50,000 tons, a thick armoured belt and a main armament of eight 15in guns, they were certainly powerful, but their lack of effective radar limited their usefulness. The sinking of the *Bismarck* in May 1941 led to the dramatic curtailment of long-range offensive operations by Germany's remaining capital ships.

KMS *Graf Spee*

## SPECIFICATIONS: *BISMARCK*

**Launched:** 14 February 1939

**Length:** 250.5m (822ft)

**Beam:** 36m (118ft)

**Draught:** 0.2m (8in)

**Displacement:** 50,900 tons (fully laden)

**Max speed:** 30.8 knots

**Max range:** 8,500 nautical miles

**Armament:** 8x 38cm guns, 12x 15cm guns, 14x

10.5cm flak guns, 16x 3.7cm flak guns, 20x 2cm

flak guns

**Crew:** 103 officers, 1,989 enlisted men

**Fate:** Sunk, 27 May 1941

## Ship details

**Previous page:** The second of the Kriegsmarine's *panzerschiffen*, the *Graf Spee* was designed as a commerce raider, capable of outrunning any cruiser sent to chase her, with the armament to take on any cruiser she couldn't evade. In late 1939 she had a successful cruise in the Indian Ocean and South Atlantic before withdrawing into Montevideo after the inconclusive battle of the River Plate (1939). She was subsequently scuttled by her captain.

**This page:** Regarded as unsinkable, the *Bismarck* sortied into the Atlantic Ocean in May 1941, in concert with the cruiser *Prinz Eugen*. At the battle of the Denmark Strait she destroyed the battlecruiser *Hood* and damaged the battleship *Prince of Wales*, before escaping into the Atlantic. She was eventually located and then damaged by a torpedo hit during an air attack. On 27 May *Bismarck* was sunk by a British task force.

KMS *Bismarck*

# BRITISH COASTAL FORCES

While the principal warring powers used small torpedo boats during World War I, these craft really came into their own after 1939. During the interwar years the British Admiralty largely ignored the development of these craft. Instead it relied on private shipbuilding companies such as Fairmile, Vosper and British Power Boat (BPB) to design boats which were then evaluated by the Royal Navy. If they proved successful a limited number were ordered. These three companies developed different types of craft. Vosper and BPB designed small, fast torpedo-armed craft, designed to attack larger enemy ships, and by contrast Fairmile vessels were larger and slower – ideal craft to defend coastal convoys from German torpedo boats or E-boats.

Britain entered World War II with a limited number of 'Coastal Forces' boats, including Coastal Motor Boats (CMBs) and Motor Launches (MLs) dating from World War I. The fall of France in 1940 led to the establishment of German E-boat bases on the French, Belgian and Dutch coasts, within easy reach of Britain's coastal shipping lanes in the North Sea and the English Channel. The small number of MLs protected the convoys alongside minesweepers and hastily converted trawlers, while the small number of Vosper and BPB Motor Torpedo Boats (MTBs) ventured across the Channel to attack German convoys. By then Coastal Forces boats had also seen action in the Mediterranean. A new shipbuilding initiative was launched, and by early 1941 the number and range of Coastal Forces craft had increased dramatically. These new vessels included Motor Gun Boats (MGBs), designed to counter enemy coastal forces, while MTBs became better armed and more versatile.

These vessels saw extensive service during the war, particularly in home waters and in the Mediterranean. As the war progressed new and ever more powerful vessels joined the fleet, including the successful Fairmile D design – a combined MGB and MTB. The powerful little warships of British Coastal Forces proved invaluable in winning control of Europe's coastal waters during the war.

# SPECIFICATIONS: MTB-223

**Built:** 1941, Scotland

**Launched:** February 1942

**Length:** 22m (72ft 6in)

**Beam:** 5.8m (19ft 2in)

**Draught:** 1.9m (6ft 3in)

**Displacement:** 40 tons

**Propulsion:** Three Packard engines

**Max speed:** 39 knots

**Armament:** 1x twin .5in MG turret, 2x .303in machine guns, 2x DCs, 2x 21in torpedo tubes.

(Note: armament varied throughout the war, but by 1944 most remaining boats had 1x twin Oerlikon aft, 1x Oerlikon, 1x 2pdr in lieu of the .5in)

**Crew:** 13

**Fate:** Scrapped, 1944

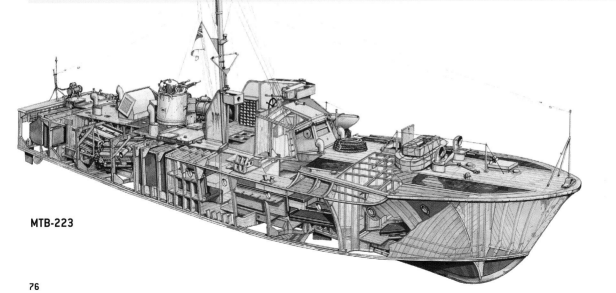

MTB-223

## Ship details

**Previous page:** The 22m (72ft) Vosper MTB was the mainstay of Britain's Coastal Forces during the early and middle years of the war. Her job was to launch torpedo attacks against enemy shipping, usually under cover of darkness. She would approach a convoy as silently as she could, launch her torpedoes, crash start her engines and – ideally – make off before the enemy could target her.

**This page:** A Fairmile D MGB, this powerful vessel was launched in 1944 and served in both home waters and the Mediterranean. Her powerful armament included a large 6pdr gun, as well as an array of lighter automatic weapons. These 'Dog Boats' were versatile little warships, and MGB-624 was used as an escort, an attack boat and to carry out 'special' operations.

MGB-624

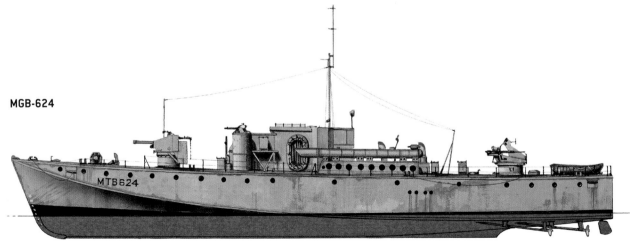

# GERMAN CRUISERS

After the end of World War I, the German Navy surrendered all its modern cruisers to the Allies, leaving just a small flotilla of vessels built before 1905, which were either broken up or used as training ships. Under the terms of the Treaty of Versailles, Germany was allowed to build a small squadron of light cruisers, displacing less than 6,000 tons. The first of these – the *Emden* – entered service in 1925, but she was followed by three larger K class vessels – *Königsberg*, *Karlsruhe* and *Köln* – which joined the Reichsmarine in 1929–30. *Leipzig* and *Nürnberg* followed during the early 1930s. These last cruisers were considerably more powerful than their predecessors, and carried nine 150mm (6in) guns in three triple turrets.

The plan to expand the Kriegsmarine led to the development of an even more powerful light cruiser. These Hipper Class warships were soon redesigned as heavy cruisers, carrying eight 8in guns. The first of these Hipper Class heavy cruisers – *Admiral Hipper* and *Blücher* – were launched in 1937, and completed two years later. By then three more heavy cruisers were being built, although only one of them – *Prinz Eugen* – finally entered service. In terms of appearance these heavy cruisers looked like small versions of the Bismarck Class.

The damage to *Leipzig* and *Nürnberg* by torpedoes in late 1939 and the sinking of *Königsberg*, *Karlsruhe* and *Blücher* during the Norwegian campaign of April 1940 cut the size of the German cruiser fleet by more than half. After that the surviving light cruisers were withdrawn from front-line service. As for the heavy cruisers, *Prinz Eugen* accompanied *Bismarck* during her sortie in May 1941 and participated in the Channel Dash, while *Admiral Hipper* was based in Norway and used to attack the Arctic convoys. With the exception of *Nürnberg* and *Prinz Eugen*, the remaining cruisers were sunk or scuttled during or immediately after the end of the war. In 1946 the surviving light cruiser was handed over to the Soviet Union, while *Prinz Eugen* was used as a target for atomic bomb testing.

**KMS *Königsberg***

# SPECIFICATIONS: *PRINZ EUGEN*

**Built:** 1936

**Launched:** 22 August 1938

**Length:** 207.7m (681ft 5in)

**Beam:** 21.9m (71ft 10in)

**Draught:** 7.95m (25ft 11in)

**Displacement:** 19,042 tons

**Max speed:** 32 knots

**Range:** 6,500 nautical miles

**Armament:** 8x 20.3cm guns in 4 twin turrets, 12x 10.5cm guns in 6 twin turrets, 12x 3.7cm guns in 6 twin turrets, 8x 2cm guns on single mounts, 12x 53.3cm torpedo tubes in 4 triple mounts

**Crew:** 50 officers and 1,500 enlisted men

**Fate:** Capsized and sank, 22 December 1946 (from atomic bomb testing).

# Ship details

**Previous page:** Commissioned in April 1929, *Königsberg* was the first of Germany's 'modern' light cruisers, armed with nine 150mm guns and a pair of 88mm anti-aircraft guns. During the war she conducted minesweeping operations in the North Sea, before participating in the invasion of Norway. On 10 April 1940 she was sunk in Bergen harbour by Fleet Air Arm Skua dive-bombers operating from Kirkwall in Orkney.

**This page:** The third of the Hipper Class to enter service, *Prinz Eugen* is best remembered for her involvement in Operation *Rheinübung* – the breakout of the battleship *Bismarck* into the Atlantic – and the part she played in the destruction of HMS *Hood*. After parting company with the battleship she sailed on to Brest, and from there she accompanied *Scharnhorst* and *Gneisenau* in the Channel Dash from Brest to Kiel.

KMS *Prinz Eugen*

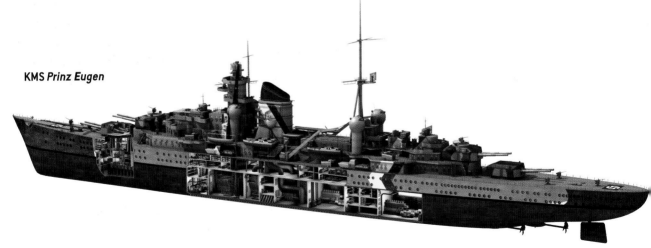

# GERMAN DESTROYERS

The Treaty of Versailles allowed Germany to retain a single flotilla of 12 destroyers. However, her surviving destroyers all predated World War I and were considered obsolete. The vessels were duly redesignated as torpedo boats, which left Germany without any seagoing destroyers. In 1934, when the limits imposed by the Treaty of Versailles were relaxed, plans were drawn up for a new destroyer flotilla. Dubbed the 1934 Type, these vessels were originally designed to conduct limited operations in the North Sea and the Baltic, but during the war German destroyers would operate as far north as the Arctic Sea.

The first batch of Type 1934 destroyers (Z-1 to Z-4) were launched in late 1935, and commissioned in 1937. By then a modified version known as the Type 1934A was under construction, which was 2 metres (6ft 6in) longer and therefore considered better suited to the harsher waters of the Norwegian Sea. The 12 destroyers of this batch were designated Z-5 to Z-16, and were launched during 1936–37. By then the first Type 1934

destroyers had been evaluated and it was decided to alter the design again, making the vessels 4 metres (13ft 2in) longer than the Type 1934As. In all, six of these new Type 1936 destroyers were launched during 1937–38. All of these three batches of destroyers had a similar appearance and were armed with five 127mm (5.1in) guns and eight torpedo tubes. Unlike the destroyers that followed them, they were given both pendant number designations and names (eg Z-2 – KMS *Georg Thiele*).

Another eight destroyers were planned to follow, but these were reconfigured to carry four 150mm (6in) guns and were redesignated as Type 1936A destroyers, numbered Z-23 to Z-30. They are sometimes incorrectly referred to as the Narvik Class. Germany entered World War II with 21 seagoing destroyers, but the loss of 12 of these off Narvik, Norway in 1940 prompted the building of replacements. Designated the Type 1936A (Mob) Class, Z-31 to Z-39 entered service in 1942–44. A final group, the four destroyers of the Type 1936B batch, were given 127mm guns and entered service during 1943–45.

**Z-1 KMS** *Leberecht Maas*

## SPECIFICATIONS: Z-39

**Launched:** 5 August 1941

**Commissioned:** 21 August 1943

**Length:** 127m (416ft 8in)

**Beam:** 12m (39ft 4in)

**Draught:** 4.5m (14ft 9in)

**Displacement:** 3,691 tons

**Max speed:** 38 knots

**Max range:** 2,500 nautical miles

**Armament:** 4x 15cm guns, 8x 3.7cm guns, 5x 2cm guns, 8x 53.3 torpedo tubes, up to 70 mines carried

**Crew:** 332

**Fate:** Scrapped, 1964

**Z-39**

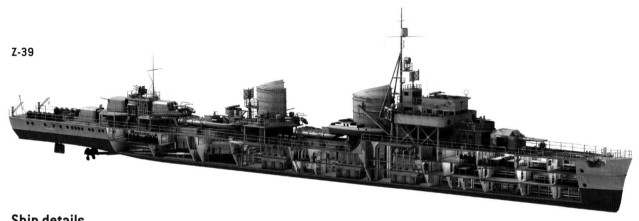

## Ship details

**Previous page:** The original batch of seagoing destroyers in the Kriegsmarine, the four vessels of the Type 1934 Class (also known as the Leberecht Maas Class) served as the blueprint for all subsequent German destroyers. They were improved themselves, as the hulls were stiffened and the bow altered. In February 1940, Z-1 and Z-3 were sunk by German bombers in a 'friendly fire' incident off the German North Sea coast.

**This page:** The Z-39 was a Type 1936A (mob) Class destroyer – the 'mob' standing for Germany's mobilization shipbuilding programme. These were the most modern and streamlined of the German wartime destroyers, and were armed with five 150mm guns and eight 555mm torpedo tubes. Z-39 was commissioned in January 1944, but was damaged that summer and only returned to service in early 1945. She survived the war and was sold to France in 1947.

# JAPANESE CARRIERS

The Washington Naval Treaty (1922) established a tonnage ratio of 5-5-3 for the British, American and Japanese capital ships, and a cap of 81,000 tons on Japanese aircraft carriers. Until then the Japanese had concentrated on conventional warships, and that year they commissioned the world's first custom-built aircraft carrier. Named *Hosho*, she carried 21 aircraft and, unusually, had no superstructure – her flight deck covered her entire upper deck. Capital ships designed to be scrapped under the terms of the treaty were then converted into aircraft carriers, the first of them being the *Akagi* and *Kaga*, which entered service during the late 1920s. Unlike the *Hosho* they were fitted with small islands amidships. They were also larger than their predecessor, carrying 66–72 aircraft apiece. These three warships formed the basis of what would become the most powerful carrier fleet in the world by the time Japan entered World War II.

By 1930 the Japanese had begun to resent the treaty restrictions, and during the 1930s the size of the carrier fleet expanded dramatically. The light carrier *Ryujo* was completed in 1933, and then, abandoning treaty limitations, the Japanese launched the *Soryu* and *Hiryu*, as well as modernizing the *Akagi* and *Kaga*.

Other carriers soon followed. In 1937 the *Zuikaku* and *Shokaku* were commissioned, designed to carry 73–84 aircraft each. The light carriers *Zuiho* and *Shoho* were converted from submarine tenders, and entered service in 1940–41. Other carriers were planned, but only the *Taiho* was ever completed. In December 1941 six carriers launched a pre-emptive strike against Pearl Harbor, and the Pacific War began. *Shoho* was sunk at the battle of the Coral Sea in April 1941, and a month later *Akagi, Kaga, Hiryu* and *Soryu* were sunk at Midway. After that the depleted Japanese carrier fleet fought a long rearguard action, trying unsuccessfully to stem the American tide in the Pacific. Eventually all but one of the carriers would be lost in action. The exception was the *Hosho*, which ended the war as a training ship.

IJNS *Akagi*

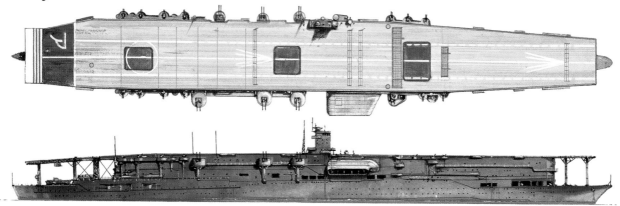

# SPECIFICATIONS: *ZUIKAKU*

**Built:** 1937

**Commissioned:** 1941

**Length:** 257.6m (845ft)

**Beam:** 26m (85ft)

**Draught:** 8.8m (29ft)

**Displacement:** 26,675 tons

**Max speed:** 34 knots

**Range:** 9,700 nautical miles

**Armaments:** 8x Type 89 mounts, 4x Type 94 fire-control systems, 18x 25mm triple mounts, 42x

single mounts, 6x 28-barrel 4.7in rocket launchers, 45x Type 91 torpedoes, 60x 1,760lb, 60x 1,100lb, 312x 550lb, 528x 132lb, 48x 66lb bombs

**Crew:** 1,800

**Fate:** Sunk, 25 October 1944

# Ship details

**Previous page:** The 37,000 ton *Akagi* (meaning 'Red Castle') was named after a Japanese mountain, and was the navy's first large aircraft carrier. In 1941 she became the flagship of the Carrier Strike Force, and saw action at Pearl Harbor, the Dutch East Indies and the Indian Ocean. She was badly damaged by American aircraft during the battle of Midway, and was scuttled on 5 June 1942.

**This page:** The *Zuikaku* and her sister ship *Shokaku* entered service shortly before Japan entered the war, and both saw service at Pearl Harbor, the Dutch East Indies and the Indian Ocean. *Zuikaku* missed the debacle at Midway but went on to participate in the carrier battles of the Coral Sea, Eastern Solomons, Santa Cruz and the Philippine Sea. She was eventually sunk by American aircraft in October 1944.

IJNS *Zuikaku*

# AMERICAN CARRIERS

The first aircraft carriers were developed during World War I, but the US Navy remained unenthusiastic about naval aviation. In 1919, the navy's Chief of Operations declared that he couldn't conceive of any use for it, and opposed plans to build aircraft carriers. Fortunately others were less reactionary, and the same year it was decided to convert the collier *Jupiter* into a carrier. She was renamed the *Langley* and entered service in 1922. By then the decision was made to convert two unwanted battlecruisers into aircraft carriers, and these were commissioned into service in 1927 as the *Lexington* and *Saratoga*. These three carriers were the foundation of a US naval carrier fleet that within two decades would become the largest naval aviation force in the world.

By December 1941, the *Langley* had been rebuilt as a seaplane tender, but the remaining two carriers had been joined by the *Yorktown*, *Ranger* and *Enterprise*. Two more – *Hornet* and *Wasp* – were nearing completion. By 1945, 22 fleet carriers (CVs) had been built, as well as nine small fleet carriers (CVLs) and 120 small escort carriers, for a total of 151 vessels.

For the first 18 months of World War II the US Navy struggled to contain the powerful Japanese carrier fleet, but after the carrier battles at Midway, the Coral Sea, the Eastern Solomons and Santa Cruz the tide had turned. By 1943 the US carrier fleet was powerful enough to take the war to the enemy. They were used to launch carrier raids against Japanese ships and bases, protect amphibious landing operations and counter any moves made by the dwindling force of Japanese carriers. As the war progressed, the US Navy gained experience in naval aviation and carrier operations, and by war's end it had evolved into a force of incredible power. There was now no question whatsoever that the aircraft carrier rather than the big gun battleship was the arbiter of victory at sea. Nowhere was this truer than in the Pacific, where the US carrier fleet was the principal architect of victory over Japan.

USS *Enterprise*

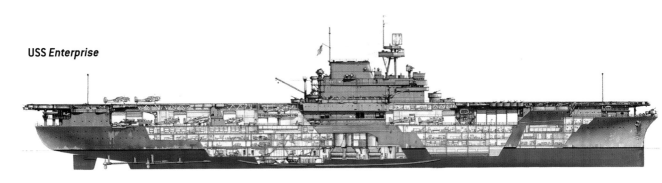

## SPECIFICATIONS: USS *ENTERPRISE*

**Built:** 1934

**Launched:** October 1936

**Commissioned:** May 1938

**Length:** 247m (810ft)

**Beam:** 33.5m (110ft)

**Draught:** 7.6m (25ft)

**Displacement:** 25,500 tons (fully loaded)

**Max speed:** 33 knots

**Range:** 11,200 nautical miles at 15 knots

**Armament:** 32x 20mm guns, 6x quadruple 40mm mounts, 8x twin 40mm mounts, 48x 20mm guns, 2x Mark 37 Directors

**Crew:** 227 officers, 1,990 enlisted men

**Fate:** Sold for scrap, 1958

USS *Ticonderoga*

## Ship details

**Previous page:** The Yorktown Class carrier *Enterprise* entered service in 1938 and fought through the entire Pacific War, taking part in more actions than any other US warships. The 'Big E' fought at Midway, the Eastern Solomons and Santa Cruz, and went on to participate in the battles of the Philippine Sea and Leyte Gulf. She was finally decommissioned in 1947 and scrapped in 1958.

**This page:** One of 14 Essex Class fleet carriers to be built during the war, *Ticonderoga* was laid down in early 1943 and entered service in May 1944. In November and December 1944 she took part in operations off the Philippines, but in January she was badly damaged by a kamikaze strike to the south of Okinawa. She survived and remained in service until 1975.

# ALLIED SUBMARINES

Among the Allies of World War II there was an increased enthusiasm for submarines following the success of German U-boats. While both the US Navy and the Royal Navy had built submarines before and during the war, experience led to a change of priorities. In America, priorities were reversed, and performance on the surface rather than under water was given a greater emphasis, given the improved range needed by US submarines operating in the Pacific. In Britain range was also considered important, hence the development of interwar 'overseas' boats of the O, P and R classes. In the Thames Class surface speed was increased at the expense of diving capability, while the Swordfish and Shark classes were built as coastal submarines, but proved so effective that they were developed into the improved T and U classes. During the war these small diesel-electric boats performed extremely well, particularly in the Mediterranean.

In the US the Pike and Perch classes produced during the 1930s were ideally suited for service in the Pacific, as they had a range of 10,000 miles. With a surface speed of 20 knots and a little under 9 knots when submerged, these diesel-electric boats proved greatly superior to the US Navy's earlier submarines. Strangely, their main propulsive power was electric – the diesel engine was there to provide power to the generators. By contrast the British boats – like German U-boats – used diesel engines on the surface and electric power when submerged. Subsequent classes of US submarines were effectively improved versions of these interwar boats. Their development culminated in the Gato Class of 1941, which had a range of 11,000 miles and could remain on patrol for 75 days. The Gato Class was mass produced in American shipyards, and from 1943 American submarines were operating in sufficient numbers to play an important part in the Pacific by causing havoc in Japan's far-flung supply lanes. While British submarines were used to harass the enemy, American boats were numerous enough to fulfil a strategic role in the Pacific War.

**Balao Class**

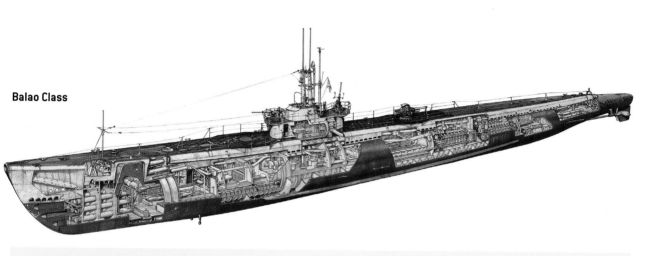

# SPECIFICATIONS: USS *BOWFIN*

**Built:** July 1942

**Launched:** December 1942

**Commissioned:** May 1943

**Length:** 95m (311ft 9in)

**Beam:** 8.31m (27ft 3in)

**Draught:** 5.13m (16ft 10in)

**Displacement:** 2,453 tons (submerged)

**Max speed:** 20.3 knots (surfaced), 8.75 knots (submerged)

**Range:** 11,000 nautical miles at 10 knots (surfaced)

**Armament:** 18x Mark 14 torpedoes

**Crew:** 66 (6 officers, 60 enlisted men)

**Fate:** Decommissioned in February 1947, recommissioned during the Korean War before being taken off the Navy list in December 1971. Now serves as a memorial at Pearl Harbor.

# Ship details

**Previous page:** The Balao Class of 122 boats was the largest class of submarines built for the US Navy during World War II. They were an improved version of the earlier Gato Class, with a greater speed and diving capability. They proved invaluable during the war, as their reliability, range and endurance meant they could reach virtually anywhere in the Pacific. Today, eight surviving Balao Class boats are preserved as museum ships.

**This page:** The British T Class (or Triton Class) was produced from 1935 onwards as an improved version of the Shark Class of coastal submarine. They had a heavy bow armament of eight external 21in torpedo tubes, which permitted a 'shotgun salvo' to be fired. A total of 53 of these boats were built before the end of hostilities and they fought in all theatres of war.

**T Class**

# JAPANESE BATTLESHIPS

While Japan embraced the potential of naval aviation, it also placed a heavy reliance on battleships. The core of this fleet were the dreadnoughts and battlecruisers built by Japan during World War I. Those that weren't converted into aircraft carriers or scrapped under the terms of the Washington Naval Treaty (1922) were modernized, making them the equal of the British or American battleships. The four Kongo Class battlecruisers, *Kongo, Hiei, Kirishima* and *Haruna*, were given sufficient armour to turn them into battleships, and their engines were improved to cope with the additional weight. The result was a class of four fast and powerful battleships, armed with eight 14in guns apiece.

The two Fuso Class battleships, *Fuso* and *Yamashiro*, were slower, but carried 12 14in guns each, which made them useful enough to retain in the battle fleet until World War II. They were distinguishable by their high pagoda-like superstructures. The dreadnoughts *Ise* and *Hyuga* were similarly armed and protected, but in 1942 the decision was made to convert them into hybrid battleship-carriers. The after turrets were removed and replaced with a flight deck, but this made them inadequate in either role. More successful were the two Nagato Class battleships, *Nagato* and *Mutsu*, completed in 1920–21. They had a belt armour of almost 12in and carried eight 16in guns each, making them the equal of the latest American battleships of the interwar years.

Shortly before the war began the Japanese launched their last two battleships – and by far the largest. These were the two vessels of the Yamato Class, *Yamato* and *Musashi*, which were sleek, modern and protected by a 16in armoured belt. They were armed with nine 18in guns, making them arguably the most powerful battleships of the war. While they lacked the radar fire control of their American counterparts, their size made them formidable adversaries. However, both of these battleships were sunk in 1944–45 – in fact all ten of Japan's wartime battleships were lost during the war.

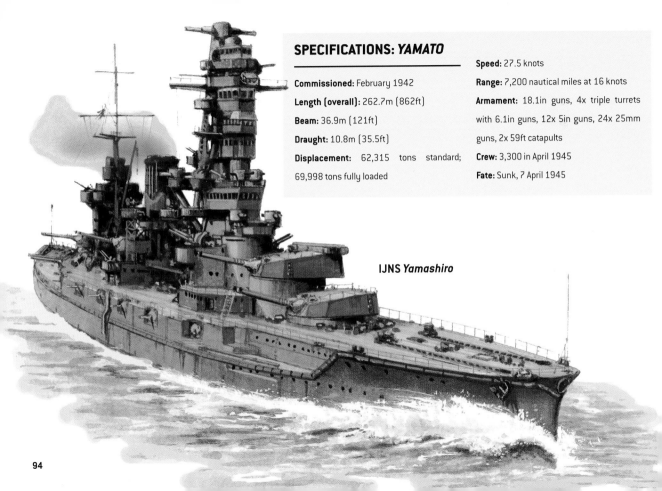

## SPECIFICATIONS: *YAMATO*

**Commissioned:** February 1942

**Length (overall):** 262.7m (862ft)

**Beam:** 36.9m (121ft)

**Draught:** 10.8m (35.5ft)

**Displacement:** 62,315 tons standard; 69,998 tons fully loaded

**Speed:** 27.5 knots

**Range:** 7,200 nautical miles at 16 knots

**Armament:** 18.1in guns, 4x triple turrets with 6.1in guns, 12x 5in guns, 24x 25mm guns, 2x 59ft catapults

**Crew:** 3,300 in April 1945

**Fate:** Sunk, 7 April 1945

**IJNS *Yamashiro***

# Ship details

**Previous page:** Commissioned during World War I, *Yamashiro* was modernized during the early 1930s, when she was given her distinctive pagoda-shaped superstructure. However, by 1941 she was considered too old and poorly armed to take on American battleships, so was relegated to secondary duties. However, in October 1944 she took part in the battle of Leyte Gulf, and was eventually sunk by American battleships and destroyers in the Surigao Strait.

**This page:** Commissioned just a week after the Pearl Harbor attack, *Yamato* became the flagship of Admiral Yamamoto, commander of the Japanese Combined Fleet. After Midway she remained in readiness to spearhead a counter-attack against any American thrust towards Japan, but she saw no real action until the battle of Leyte Gulf in October 1944. She was eventually sunk off Okinawa by American aircraft in April 1945.

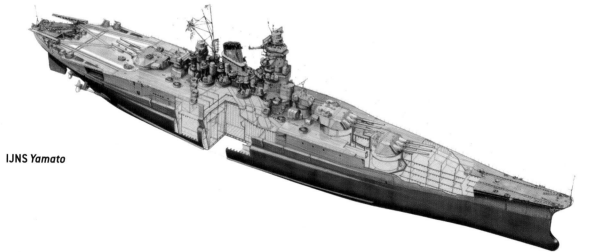

IJNS *Yamato*

# BRITISH BATTLESHIPS

The Washington Naval Treaty (1922) led to the dismantling of Britain's dreadnought fleet. The 'fast battleships' of the Queen Elizabeth and Royal Sovereign classes survived, though, as their 15in guns were considered too useful to allow these capital ships to be scrapped. The parsimony of the interwar years meant that improvements to their design came slowly, but to a greater or lesser extent all five Queen Elizabeths and four Royal Sovereigns were modified during the interwar years. All of them had their twin funnels combined into one and the superstructures of the *Queen Elizabeth* and her two sisters, *Warspite* and *Valiant*, were extensively rebuilt. These ageing battleships all played a significant part in World War II, despite the loss of *Barham* in 1941 and damage inflicted on her three sisters. *Warspite* in particular had a remarkable wartime career, seeing action off Norway, in the Mediterranean, the Pacific and off Normandy. The slower and less well-protected Royal Sovereigns were considered less useful, and were largely relegated to second-line duties. All survived the war with the exception of *Royal Oak*, which was torpedoed in Scapa Flow in 1939.

In 1922 the two Nelson Class battleships, *Nelson* and *Rodney*, were laid down, and both had distinguished wartime careers. Despite their ungainly appearance their armament of nine 16in guns in three triple turrets made them extremely potent warships. The most modern wartime group of British battleships were the five vessels of the King George V Class. Completed between 1940 and 1942 they proved their worth against the *Bismarck* and *Scharnhorst*, and despite their smaller calibre armament of ten 14in guns their suite of search and fire-control radars made them powerful adversaries. The *Duke of York* relied on her radar fire control to sink the German battlecruiser *Scharnhorst* in the battle of North Cape (1943). What let all British battleships down was their anti-aircraft capability. However, after *Prince of Wales* was sunk by Japanese aircraft off Malaya in 1941, all remaining battleships were given an improved array of light anti-aircraft weaponry.

## SPECIFICATIONS:
## HMS *WARSPITE*

**Built:** 1912, Devonport

**Launched:** 26 November 1913

**Commissioned:** March 1915

**Length (overall):** 196.8m (645ft 9in)

**Beam:** 27.6m (90ft 6in)

**Draught:** 8.8m (28ft 9in)

**Displacement:** 31,315 tons

**Propulsion:** 4 Parsons turbines, 6 Admiralty boilers producing 80,000hp

**Max speed:** 24 knots

**Armament:** 8x 15in Mark I BL guns, 8x 6in guns, 8x 4in anti-aircraft guns, 4x 8in barrelled 2pdr 'pom-poms', 4x quad machine guns

**Crew:** 950

**Fate:** Broken up in 1947

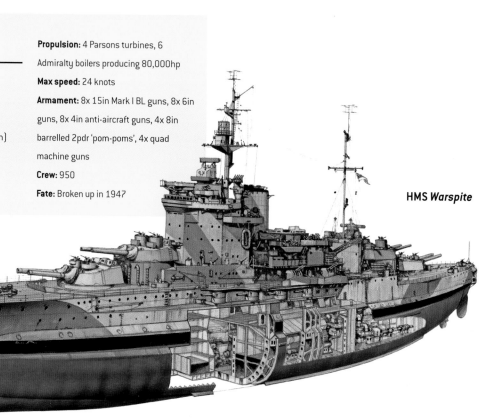

HMS *Warspite*

# Ship details

**Previous page:** Probably the most famous British battleship of World War II, *Warspite* was commissioned in 1915 and took part in the battle of Jutland (1916). She was modernized between the wars, and in World War II fought at Narvik, Calabria and Matapan, and fired in support of landings in Sicily, Salerno, Normandy and Walcheren. Although badly damaged three times she survived the war and was decommissioned in 1945.

**This page:** The two battleships of the Nelson Class looked very ungainly due to their truncated appearance. This was due to the limitations of the Washington Naval Treaty – the ships were designed to make full use of every ton of displacement, which made *Rodney* as powerful as she was ugly. In 1941 her 16in guns helped sink the *Bismarck*, and she took part in shore bombardments in the Mediterranean and off Normandy.

HMS *Rodney*

# AMERICAN DESTROYERS

**B**y the end of World War I, the US Navy had a large destroyer fleet, but many of these were scrapped following the Washington Naval Treaty (1922) and the scaling down of the navy. By the 1930s most of these older 'flush decked' destroyers were considered obsolete, and were either decommissioned or converted into minelayers, minesweepers, fast troop transports or seaplane tenders. The introduction of powerful Japanese destroyers during the 1930s led to a demand for a matching fleet of modern American destroyers. Consequently the Porter, Mahan and Gridley classes were developed, armed with a combination of 5in guns and torpedoes.

Rather than matching the Japanese in terms of quality, the US Navy decided to make their destroyers smaller but more numerous than their rivals in the Pacific. While vessels like the new Benson Class carried a similar armament to their predecessors, they were also designed to take full advantage of technological improvements in anti-submarine detection and weaponry. By 1941 the US Navy had just over 100 modern destroyers, a quarter of which were the latest Benson and Greaves classes. They were less well armed than their Japanese counterparts, so the navy decided to build a new group of larger vessels. These Fletcher, Allen M. Sumner and Gearing class destroyers were all laid down between 1941 and 1944, and while 331 of them were built, almost a third were completed after the end of hostilities. Some weren't commissioned until the late 1950s.

Despite the Japanese advantage in firepower and torpedo armament, the pre-war destroyers acquitted themselves well during the hard-fought naval battles around Guadalcanal and then elsewhere in the Solomon Islands. American destroyers were versatile warships, called upon to perform a range of duties, from task force escort, anti-submarine patrolling, fighting in surface action groups, performing naval bombardment and operating in direct support of amphibious landings. They were literally the workhorses of the war in the Pacific, and victory would have been impossible without them.

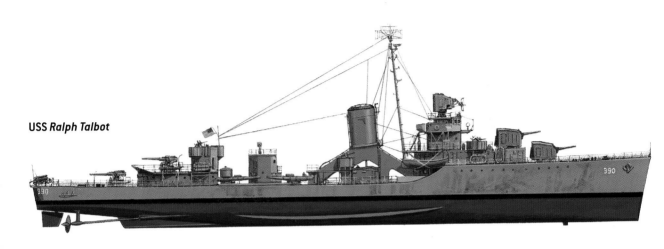

USS *Ralph Talbot*

## SPECIFICATIONS:
## USS *RALPH TALBOT*

**Built:** October 1935

**Launched:** October 1936

**Commissioned:** 1937

**Length (overall):** 104m (341ft 4in)

**Beam:** 10.67m (34ft 12in)

**Draught:** 5.2m (17ft 1in)

**Displacement:** 1,500 tons

**Propulsion:** 2 propellers, 49,000shp

**Max speed:** 35.5 knots

**Range:** 5,520 nautical miles at 12 knots

**Armament:** 4x 5in/38cal guns, 4x .50cal machine guns, 12x 21in torpedo tubes

**Crew:** 158 (8 officers, 150 men)

**Fate:** Decommissioned, August 1946; sunk, March 1948

# Ship details

**Previous page:** The Bagley Class destroyer *Ralph Talbot* was typical of the US destroyers built during the 1930s. She only carried four 5in guns, but she boasted a powerful battery of 12 21in torpedoes, mounted in three quadruple launchers. Although badly damaged at the battle of Savo Island she survived and fought in several more surface actions before the end of the war.

**This page:** The Allen M. Sumner Class destroyer *Laffey* was commissioned in 1944, the second US destroyer to bear the name. She was typical of the powerful five-gun American destroyers built during the war, and she saw service off Okinawa, where she was damaged during a kamikaze attack. She remained in service until 1975 when she became a museum ship, berthed in Charleston, South Carolina.

USS *Laffey*

# AMERICAN FAST BATTLESHIPS

Under the terms of the Washington Naval Treaty of 1922 the US Navy's fleet of dreadnoughts was culled slightly, but by 1931 ten former dreadnoughts (or 'standard type' battleships) remained in service, while two more served as target ships. Another group of capital ships was completed after World War I, built along more modern lines. These included two battleships of the Tennessee Class and three of the Colorado Class. All other American battleships or battlecruisers laid down before the treaty were cancelled, apart from the two battlecruisers which were converted into aircraft carriers. This still left a sizeable force of 15 battleships, divided between the Pacific and Atlantic fleets. Many of these old battleships were modernized during the interwar years, and as all but *Arkansas* and the Colorado Class were armed with 14in guns, they still had a role to play in any future naval war.

By 1941 *Arkansas* had been relegated to second-line service in the Atlantic fleet. However, the three Colorado Class battleships (*Colorado*, *Maryland* and *West Virginia*) carried powerful 16in guns, and these weapons were used in the next generation of American 'fast battleships', which were designed during the mid-1930s and began to enter service from 1941. These were all armed with nine 16in guns, mounted in three triple turrets. By 1941–42 they were fitted with radar and radar-guided fire-control systems, which made them more than a match for their Japanese counterparts. During the attack on Pearl Harbor in December 1941, four US battleships were sunk, while another four were either damaged or forced aground. Of these the *Arizona* was a total loss, and while *Oklahoma*, *West Virginia* and *California* were raised, only the last two were recommissioned into service. The remaining four had rejoined the fleet by 1942. While these and the 'fast battleships' carried out vital naval bombardment missions during the 'island hopping' campaign in the Pacific, aircraft carriers rather than battleships were now the principal capital ships of the fleet, and these great battlewagons became the last of their kind.

## SPECIFICATIONS: USS
## *NORTH CAROLINA*

**Built:** 1937, New York

**Launched:** 13 June 1940

**Commissioned:** 9 April 1941

**Length (overall):** 222m (728ft 8in)

**Beam:** 33m (108ft 3in)

**Draught:** 17.2m (35ft 6in)

**Displacement:** 44,800 tons (fully loaded
– 1942), 46,700 tons (fully loaded –
1945)

**Max speed (1941):** 28 knots

**Range (1941):** 17,450 nautical miles at
15 knots

**Armament (1941):** 9x 16in/45cal guns
(Mark 6), 20x 5in/38cal guns (Mark 12),
16x 1.1in AA guns, 40x 20mm AA guns,
12x .50cal AA guns

**Crew:** 1,880

**Fate:** Decommissioned in 1947;
dedicated as a war memorial at
Wilmington, 3 October 1961.

**USS *North Carolina***

# Ship details

**Previous page:** The first of the US Navy's fast battleships, *North Carolina* entered service in April 1941 and served briefly with the Atlantic fleet before being sent to the Pacific. She saw action off Guadalcanal and supported carrier operations in the South Pacific, before using her guns in support of landings at Palau, Saipan and Okinawa. She survived the war, and is now preserved as a museum ship near Wilmington, NC.

**This page:** The *Iowa* was the lead ship in her class of four 'fast battleships', and entered service in February 1943. She took part in operations off Saipan, the Philippines and Japan. She remained in service after the war and saw action during the Korean and Vietnam wars. She was decommissioned in 1958, but was briefly restored to service between 1984 and 1990. She is now preserved as a museum ship in San Pedro.

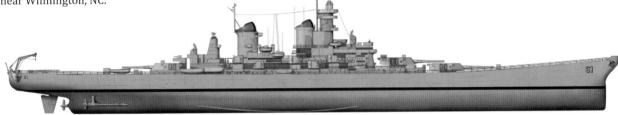

**USS *Iowa***

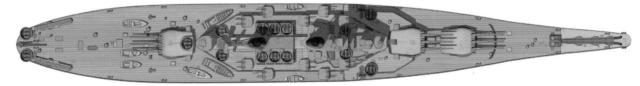

# JAPANESE HEAVY CRUISERS

Although the Japanese possessed a small cruiser force by the end of World War I, many of their armoured cruisers were either scrapped or served in Chinese waters during the war. A crop of light cruisers laid down during the closing months of the war or shortly afterwards were completed between 1918 and 1925, by which time they were considered of limited use in a future naval war in the Pacific. During World War II many were relegated to escort duties. The Japanese were quick to embrace the opportunities as well as the restrictions of the Washington Naval Treaty (1922), and began building cruisers which matched the upper limits of size and armament laid out in the agreement. The first of these were the Furutaka and Aoba classes, which carried six 8in guns apiece, as well as a powerful array of torpedoes.

While these warships were still slightly smaller than the treaty limits, the next batch – the Nachi Class – were much larger and more powerful, and unofficially they exceeded the displacement restrictions of the 1922 treaty. These four heavy cruisers carried twin 8in guns each, employing a rare configuration where 'B' turret was superimposed over 'A' and 'C' turrets, which meant that 'C' turret could only fire in broadside. This basic design was repeated in the four heavy cruisers of the Takao Class, which entered service in 1932.

The four-ship Mogami Class, which was completed in 1935–36, represented a change of direction for the Japanese: a class of four light cruisers which resembled the earlier Nachis and Takaos, but which were fitted with triple turrets, giving a total armament of 15 6in guns. A subsequent four-ship class of light cruisers – the Tone Class – were rebuilt as heavy cruisers with eight 8in guns when Japan abandoned her treaty restrictions in the mid-1930s. This large and powerful cruiser fleet proved highly effective during the early years of the war, and the heavy cruisers in particular saw extensive service in defence of the Japanese defensive cordon in the South Pacific.

IJNS *Sendai*

# SPECIFICATIONS: *AOBA*

**Built:** 1924

**Launched:** 25 September 1926

**Commissioned:** 20 September 1927

**Length (overall):** 185m (607ft 6in)

**Beam:** 17.6m (57ft 8in)

**Draught:** 10m (33ft)

**Displacement:** 11,660 tons (fully loaded)

**Speed:** 33–34 knots

**Range:** 8,223 nautical miles at 14 knots

**Armament:** 50cal Type 3 No. 2 Model C, twin 7.9in turrets, four triple and 15 single 25mm guns, five triple, ten double and 15 single 25mm guns

**Crew:** 54 officers and 626 enlisted

**Fate:** Sunk, October 1945

# Ship details

**Previous page:** The *Sendai* was the namesake of her class, a batch of four light cruisers built during the early 1920s. With her weak armament of seven 5.5in guns, *Sendai* was not regarded as a front-line warship but nevertheless she still participated in the naval battles fought in defence of Guadalcanal. In November 1943 she was sunk by American cruisers during the battle of Empress Augusta Bay in the Solomon Islands.

**This page:** Although technically the Furutakas and the Aobas were two separate classes of two ships each, effectively they were the same batch of heavy cruisers. They saw extensive service in the naval battles fought around Guadalcanal in 1942, where *Aoba* served as a squadron flagship, and was badly damaged during the battle of Cape Esperance. She rejoined the fleet in 1943, but subsequent damage meant she was removed from active service.

**IJNS *Aoba***

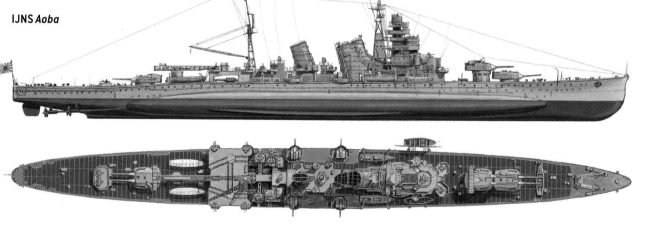

# ITALIAN BATTLESHIPS

Under the encouragement of Benito Mussolini's Fascists, the Italian Navy expanded dramatically during the interwar period. By 1940 it consisted of a well-balanced fleet, centred around its battleships. The Italians eschewed naval aviation, and instead placed their reliance on land-based aircraft to provide air cover for their surface fleet. Italy's most likely rivals were Great Britain and France, and so the battleship fleet was expected to match that of the Royal Navy's Mediterranean Fleet. Italy already had five dreadnoughts – three of the Cavour Class and two of the Doria Class, all of which were launched before the outbreak of World War I. During the 1920s and again in the mid-1930s four battleships were extensively rebuilt (the exception was the Cavour Class vessel *Leonardo da Vinci*, which didn't survive World War I) and by 1940 they were qualitatively as good as most of their equally ageing British counterparts.

The two surviving ships of the Cavour Class – *Conti di Cavour* and *Giulio Cesare* – emerged from their final pre-war refit in 1937, when they boasted a main armament of ten 305mm (12in) guns, in two twin and two triple turrets, and a powerful array of secondary guns and anti-aircraft mounts. The Doria Class battleships, *Andrea Doria* and *Caio Duilio*, carried a similar armament, and by 1940 all four ships were remarkably similar in appearance. The *Conti di Cavour* was sunk by British aircraft at Taranto in November 1940, but was subsequently raised, although never returned to active service. *Caio Duilio* and *Littorio* were also badly damaged during the attack.

During the 1930s work began on the Littorio Class of battleships, two of which – *Littorio* and *Vittorio Veneto* – entered service in 1940. A third, the *Roma*, joined the fleet in 1942. Mounting nine 381mm (16in) guns in three triple turrets, these battleships were both modern and potent. However, the timidity of the Italian command meant that their potential was never fully realized. *Roma* was sunk by the Germans following Italy's surrender, but her two sister ships survived the war.

RN *Conti di Cavour*

## SPECIFICATIONS: *VITTORIO VENETO*

**Built:** 1934, Trieste

**Launched:** 25 July 1937

**Displacement:** 45,029 tons (fully loaded)

**Length:** 237.74m (780ft)

**Beam:** 32.9m (108ft 1in)

**Draught:** 10.47m (34ft 4in)

**Max speed:** 29 knots (fully loaded)

**Range:** 3,966 nautical miles

**Armament:** 10x 15in/50cal M1934, 12x 6in/55cal M1934, 12x 3.5in/50cal M1938

**Crew:** 78–82 officers and 1,750–1,760 enlisted men

**Fate:** Scrapped, 1948–1950

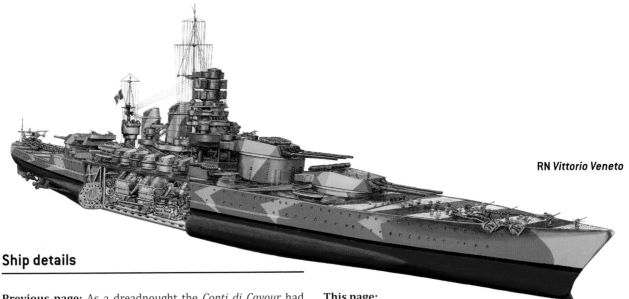

RN *Vittorio Veneto*

## Ship details

**Previous page:** As a dreadnought the *Conti di Cavour* had carried five turrets, but her mounting amidship was removed during the interwar period. In the battle of Calabria in July 1940 she flew the flag of Admiral Campione. During the Fleet Air Arm's attack on Taranto that November she was hit by a torpedo and sank. She was subsequently raised, but repairs were still being completed when Italy surrendered in September 1943.

**This page:**
The Littorio Class battleship *Vittorio Veneto* entered service in April 1940 and survived the Taranto attack to take part in the battle of Cape Spartivento. Again she emerged unscathed, but she was less fortunate off Matapan in March 1941, when she was badly damaged by a British naval air strike. Although she conducted other sorties, she never saw action again before surrendering to the Allies in September 1943.

# BRITISH CRUISERS

Like the other maritime powers between the wars, Britain's cruiser force evolved into two major groups, classified by the calibre of the ships' main armament. Light cruisers carried 6in guns or less, while heavy cruisers used larger calibre guns – mostly 8in ones. The naval treaties of 1922 and 1930 specified the type of cruiser that could be built, and consequently the Royal Navy built heavy and then light cruisers, in accordance with treaty restrictions. The heavy cruisers were given the additional task of hunting down enemy raiders, while light cruisers were tasked with convoy and task force protection. However, the Royal Navy saw the primary role of the cruiser as being the protection of maritime trade.

In 1939 Britain's cruiser force still contained 26 vessels which had been laid down during World War I, but a shortage of replacements meant that they remained in service until new ships could be built. Many of these ageing cruisers were converted into anti-aircraft escorts, or relegated to second-line duties when more modern vessels entered service. The County Class heavy cruisers built between 1924 and 1930 were commissioned in three batches, each of which differed in minor details. However, all of them were armed with eight 8in guns in four twin turrets, augmented by a secondary dual-purpose battery of 4in guns. Two additional heavy cruisers, *Exeter* and *York*, which entered service in 1930–31, only carried six 8in guns apiece.

Following the London Naval Conference (1930) Britain switched to building 6in cruisers, the first of which were the Leander and Arethusa classes, which entered service during the mid-1930s. They only carried six or eight 6in guns each due to treaty limitations. When these restrictions were abandoned, the Admiralty ordered the Southampton, Edinburgh and Fiji classes, which carried 12 6in guns, mounted in triple turrets. This formed the core of the wartime cruiser fleet, augmented from 1940 onwards by Dido and Bellona class anti-aircraft cruisers, and designed for fleet carrier group and convoy protection.

HMS *Belfast*

# SPECIFICATIONS: HMS *BELFAST*

**Built:** 1936, Belfast

**Launched:** 17 March 1938

**Commissioned:** 3 August 1939

**Length (overall):** 187m (613ft 6in)

**Beam:** 19.3m (63ft 4in)

**Draught:** 6.5m (21ft 3in)

**Displacement:** 10,550 tons

**Propulsion:** Four shaft Parsons geared turbines, four Admiralty 3-drum boilers, producing 80,000shp

**Max speed:** 32.5 knots

**Armament:** 12x 6in Mk XXIII in four triple mounts, 12x 4in Mk XVI in six double mounts, 2x 8-barrelled 2pdr 'pom-poms', 5x twin 20mm, 8x single 20mm

**Crew:** 781

**Fate:** Preserved as a museum ship, moored in the River Thames.

# Ship details

**Previous page:** Like her sister *Edinburgh*, *Belfast* was commissioned in August 1939 as part of the two-ship Edinburgh Class. These cruisers were similar to the earlier Southampton Class, but were longer, with better protection and armament. *Belfast* was damaged by a mine in 1939 but was repaired in time to play a decisive role in the battle of North Cape (1943). She is now preserved as a museum ship in London.

**This page:** Although dubbed a County Class cruiser, *Norfolk* was actually the namesake of a two-ship class of its own, as she and *Dorsetshire* formed the third and final batch of Counties to enter service. Both Norfolk Class cruisers were commissioned in 1930. *Norfolk* played an active part in the war, and was present during the destruction of both the *Bismarck* in 1941 and the *Scharnhorst* in 1943.

**HMS *Norfolk***

# JAPANESE DESTROYERS

By the end of World War I Japan had a large destroyer fleet, but most of these were considered obsolete and were either converted into minesweepers or scrapped during the late 1920s and early 1930s. They were replaced by a new design of destroyer – much larger and more powerful than their predecessors. Arguably Japan led the way in destroyer design during the interwar period, producing innovative designs that proved both powerful and versatile. The 24 ships of the Fubuki Class, completed in 1928–32, were probably the most powerful destroyers in the world when they entered service. They carried 5in guns in completely enclosed turrets, and their high angle of elevation made them as useful in an anti-aircraft role as in an anti-surface ship one. Their main armament, though, was their bank of 24in torpedoes, larger weapons than those carried by most other navies.

During the early 1930s this powerful torpedo armament was augmented when Japanese destroyers were fitted with 'Long Lance' torpedoes. These oxygen-fuelled weapons had a range of 22,000 yards – three times that of American torpedoes. Their potential was kept secret until the war began, and so their remarkable range and effectiveness came as an unpleasant surprise to the Allies. The Fubukis were followed by several smaller destroyer classes – Akizuki, Hatsuharu, Shiratsuyu, Asashio and Kagero – adding a total of 48 destroyers, all of which were in service by the time Japan entered the war. Effectively they were similar to the Fubuki Class, and designed to give the maximum performance possible while remaining within the size and armament constraints of the London Treaty of 1930. All of them carried eight or nine torpedo tubes, in triple or quadruple launchers, and a battery of five or six 5in guns. The wartime Yugumo Class followed a similar design, but the Akizukis completed during the war had a reduced torpedo armament, and carried eight 3.9in guns instead. This large destroyer fleet provided the Japanese with a potent weapon, and proved its worth during the surface actions fought off Guadalcanal and the Solomons.

IJNS *Yudachi*

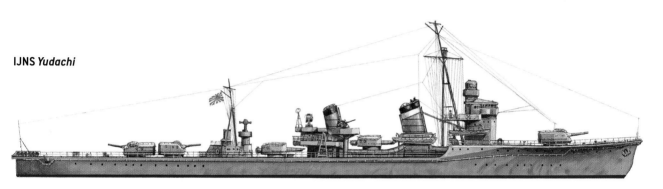

## SPECIFICATIONS: *YUGUMO*

**Built:** 1940/41

**Launched:** 16 March 1941

**Length (overall):** 119m (391ft)

**Beam:** 10.8m (35ft 6in)

**Draught:** 3.8m (12ft 4in)

**Displacement:** 2,077 tons

**Speed:** 35 knots

**Range:** 5,000 nautical miles at 18 knots

**Armament:** 6x 5in/50cal naval gun, 4x 25mm AA gun, 8x Type 92 torpedo tubes

**Crew:** 228

**Fate:** Sunk, October 1943

# Ship details

**Previous page:** The destroyer *Yudachi* entered service in early 1937, and like her nine Shiratsuyu Class sister ships she was capable of being used as an escort vessel, but her primary role was as a nocturnal hunter. The Japanese excelled in night-time destroyer tactics, and *Yudachi* formed part of the 'Tokyo Express', running supplies into Guadalcanal, but was sunk during the first battle of Guadalcanal, on 12–13 November 1942.

**This page:** The namesake of her class, *Yugumo* entered service two days before the attack on Pearl Harbor. She was used as a fast troop transport of the 'Tokyo Express' during the Guadalcanal campaign in late 1942, and elsewhere in the South Pacific throughout 1943. She was eventually sunk by American destroyers in October 1943 during the battle of Vella Lavella.

IJNS *Yugumo*

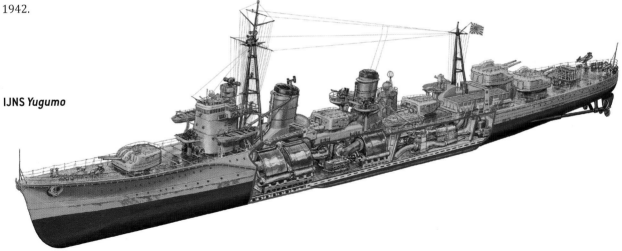

# VIETNAM RIVERINE CRAFT

During the First War in Indochina (1946–54) the French made extensive use of a 'Dinassault' flotilla of converted landing craft and other small boats to patrol the waters of French Indochina and to transport troops. This flotilla included vessels armed with gun turrets and machine guns, as well as more conventional vessels. This became the inspiration for the establishment of a similar riverine force by the United States. Originally called the Mekong Delta Mobile Afloat Force, this collection of small vessels was used as a versatile strike force, operating in the Mekong Delta. The lack of roads in this area and the sheer quantity of rivers and tributaries made it an ideal environment for this kind of warfare. The flotilla was redesignated the Mobile Riverine Force (MRF) in 1967.

The types of craft used by the MRF varied according to their function. At first, conventional landing craft were used, such as the LCM-6 'Mike Boat', but these were soon replaced by more specialist craft. Armoured troop carriers (ATCs or 'Tango Boats') served as landing craft, and were organized into four river assault groups. Command and Control Boats (CCBs) provided tactical control for river groups, while monitors armed with guns, auto-cannons, mortars and machine guns provided supporting fire. Several other types of vessel were also used in support of riverine operations, including water cannon-equipped ATCs. Patrolling was carried out by craft designated as Patrol Boat River (PBRs) and Patrol Craft Fast (PCFs or 'Swift Boats'). Assault River Patrol Boats (ASPBs or 'Alpha Boats') were used to ferry men and stores along the Mekong's waterways. All these craft were well armed – even the ATCs carried an assortment of machine guns, 20mm auto-cannons and a grenade launcher. The monitors were equipped with a similar array, as well as 40mm Bofors guns carried in armoured turrets and an 81mm mortar. Together this strange assortment of specialist riverine craft gave good service in Vietnam, both under US control and from 1970–75 when they were operated by the South Vietnamese.

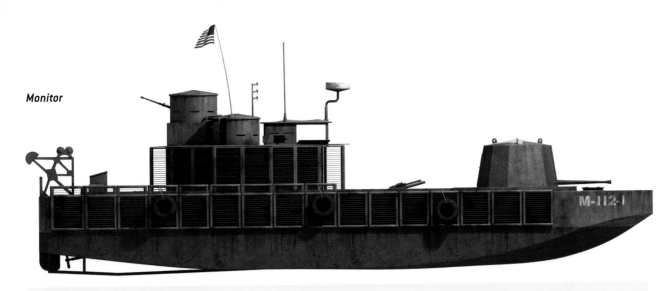

*Monitor*

M-112-1

## SPECIFICATIONS: PCF 'SWIFT BOAT'

**Built:** 1965

**Length:** 15m (50ft 1.5in)

**Beam:** 4m (13ft 1in)

**Draught:** 1.5m (5ft)

**Displacement:** 19.3 tons

**Propulsion:** Two GM diesel engines, generating 960hp

**Max speed:** 32 knots

**Range:** 320 nautical miles at 21 knots, to *c.*750 nautical miles at 10 knots

**Armament:** 2x .50cal M2 Browning machine guns, 1x 81mm mortar

**Crew:** 6

# Ship details

**Previous page:** The monitors used by the 'Brown Water Navy' in Vietnam were converted from landing craft, protected by metal sheeting and equipped with a battery of 40mm guns, auto-cannons, grenade launchers, machine guns and a mortar. In 1969 some were equipped with 105mm howitzers. As they only drew 1m (3½ft) of water they were invaluable at providing close fire support to American troops during riverine operations in the Delta.

**This page:** The Patrol Craft Fast (PCF) was an all-aluminium boat, designed in 1965 to patrol the waterways of Vietnam. They had a six-man crew, and were armed with a twin .5in machine gun in a bow mounting, plus another 0.50cal machine gun with a mortar attachment in the stern. At least 110 of these craft served in Vietnam during the war, and several of these were lost in action.

**Swift Boat**

# AMERICAN COLD WAR CARRIERS

**B**y 1945 America had become convinced that naval air power was the arbiter of victory at sea. So when World War II ended the US Navy decided to continue building the new batch of large carriers that were nearing completion. The first of these, *Midway*, entered service just eight days after the Japanese surrender. Her two Midway Class sister ships, *Frankin D. Roosevelt* and *Coral Sea*, were commissioned between 1945 and 1947. Until 1955 these 45,000 ton carriers were the largest combat vessels in the world. By then they had been converted to operate jet aircraft and soon proved their worth in Cold War exercises in the Atlantic and the Mediterranean. None of them saw service during the Korean War, but all three carriers conducted air operations off Vietnam. They were modified several times during their service careers, and were finally decommissioned in 1992.

The Korean War led to the demand for larger carriers, and so the Forrestal Class was developed as the US Navy's first true 'super carriers', designed to carry the latest forms of jet aircraft. As they displaced 75,000 tons they dwarfed the Midway Class carriers that preceded them and could carry 90 aircraft, almost twice the air complement of their predecessors. *Forrestal* entered service in 1955, and within four years she was joined by three sister ships – *Wasp*, *Saratoga* and *Independence*. They remained in service until the 1990s. However, by the time these ships were entering service, the US Navy decided to commission a new batch of vessels that were even larger.

These new super carriers, known as the Kitty Hawk Class, joined the fleet during the 1960s. The class namesake was followed by three other carriers – *Constellation*, *America* and *John F. Kennedy.* They formed the core of the US Navy's carrier force throughout the Cold War, but all have now been decommissioned. While these were being built, another experimental carrier was also being produced. She was the nuclear-powered super carrier *Enterprise*, which entered service in 1962, and remained in commission until 2012.

USS *Enterprise*

## SPECIFICATIONS:
## USS *FORRESTAL*

**Built:** 1952

**Launched:** 11 December 1954

**Commissioned:** 1 October 1955

**Length (overall):** 301.7m (990ft)

**Beam:** 39.5m (129.6ft)

**Draught:** 10.9m (36ft)

**Displacement:** 79,000 tons (fully loaded)

**Propulsion:** eight Babcock and Wilcox boilers, four

Westinghouse turbine engines, 260,000shp

**Armament:** 8x Mk 12 single-mount 5in/38cal guns

**Crew:** 4,500

**Fate:** Decommissioned, 11 September 1993. Sold

for scrap, October 2013.

# Ship details

**Previous page:** The world's first (and only) nuclear-powered aircraft carrier, the *Enterprise* was meant to be the first of a class of six nuclear carriers, but only *Enterprise* was built. She remains the longest warship in the world, and remained in commission for over 50 years, making her the longest-serving carrier in the US Navy's history. *Enterprise* had a complement of over 3,000 and could carry as many as 90 aircraft.

**This page:** *Forrestal* was the first 'super carrier' to enter service with the US Navy, joining the fleet in 1955. She was designed to carry up to 85 aircraft. She and her sister ships were used extensively during the Cold War, serving off 'hot spots' such as Cuba, Vietnam, Lebanon and the Persian Gulf. She survived two serious fires during the 1970s, underwent several refits and was finally decommissioned in 1993.

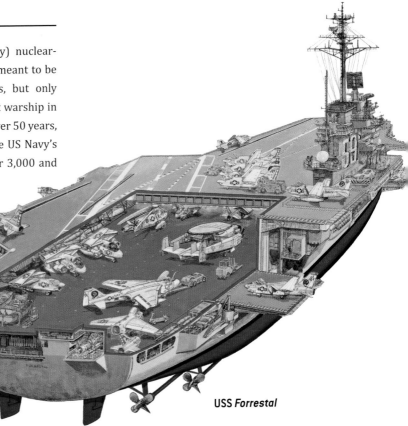

**USS *Forrestal***

# NUCLEAR SUBMARINES

In 1951 work began on a nuclear-powered submarine. The programme was supervised by Admiral Rickover, who later became known as 'the father of the nuclear navy'. He believed that nuclear energy represented the perfect power source for America's post-war submarine fleet. The US Navy's first nuclear-powered boat, the *Nautilus*, entered service in 1954. It put to sea the following January, when it sent the signal 'underway on nuclear power'. *Nautilus* demonstrated her potential by transiting the polar icecap under water and proved both dependable and efficient. The US Navy soon commissioned other nuclear-powered submarines, the first of these being the one-off *Seawolf*, followed by the Skate Class of SSNs (nuclear-powered attack submarines).

Other maritime powers followed America's lead. The Soviet Union produced its first Whale (or 'November') Class SSN in the late 1960s, while the Royal Navy's first nuclear-powered submarine, HMS *Dreadnought*, was commissioned in 1963. During the 1950s and 1960s other nuclear attack submarines followed – the Soviet Victor Class, the British Valiant Class and the US Skipjack, Thresher and Sturgeon classes. These were all 'attack submarines', whose primary job was to hunt, detect and track down enemy submarines. The advent of the ballistic-missile carrying submarine (SSBN) gave these boats a new job – protecting the SSBNs (or 'boomers') from the enemy. These were first developed by the Soviet Navy in the late 1950s and the first American SSBN, the *George Washington*, was commissioned in 1959.

During the Cold War both the US and Soviet navies maintained large fleets of both attack submarines and ballistic-missile submarines. They played a deadly game of cat and mouse in the North Atlantic, the Pacific and beneath the polar icecap, but fortunately these submarines were never called upon to fight each other for real, or to launch their nuclear missiles. The latest generation of SSNs are much stealthier than their predecessors, and more versatile, as they carry a broader array of weaponry and surveillance equipment.

USS *Nautilus*

## SPECIFICATIONS: USS *LOS ANGELES*

**Built:** January 1972

**Launched:** 6 April 1974

**Commissioned:** 13 November 1976

**Length:** 109.7m (360ft)

**Beam:** 10m (33ft)

**Displacement:** 6,000 tons (surfaced) 6,900 tons (submerged)

**Max speed:** 15 knots (surfaced), 30 knots (submerged)

**Range:** Only limited by supplies

**Armament:** 4x Mk 67 torpedo tubes

**Crew:** 127 (12 officers, 115 enlisted men)

**Fate:** Still in service

# Ship details

**Previous page:** Nuclear power transformed submarine warfare. As the world's first nuclear-powered submarine, and first 'hunter killer' (or SSN), *Nautilus* was capable of remaining submerged virtually indefinitely, and she broke world records for underwater speed and endurance. Despite her revolutionary power plant she was conventionally armed with six torpedo tubes. Although an experimental vessel, *Nautilus* remained in service until 1980, and is now a museum ship.

**This page:** The large and powerful Los Angeles Class of SSNs was introduced during the 1970s, and represented a new generation of submarine in terms of stealth, weaponry and electronics. A total of 62 Los Angeles Class boats were commissioned and most remain in service. Since entering service they have been updated with improved sensors and computer systems, and adapted to carry cruise missiles and Harpoon anti-ship missiles as well as torpedoes.

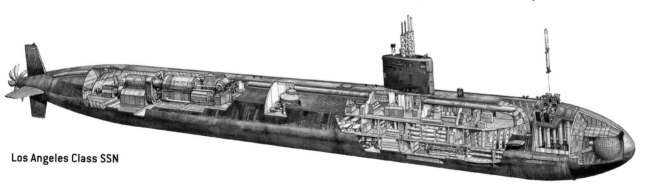

**Los Angeles Class SSN**

# AMERICAN MODERN SUPER CARRIERS

The concept of the 'super carrier' was introduced during the 1950s, as a new generation of large aircraft carriers entered service with the US Navy, designed from the keel up to operate modern jet aircraft. The Forrestal and Kitty Hawk classes, together with the *Enterprise*, formed the core of America's carrier fleet, and were numerous enough to permit the despatch of one or two 'carrier groups' to trouble spots around the world, whenever and wherever they were needed. This projection of naval air power proved a great boon to the United States during the Cold War, but by the early 1970s it was felt that a new generation of super carriers was needed in order to prolong the service life of the existing fleet. It was also felt that these should be nuclear powered. This led to the development of the Nimitz Class.

The lead ship of the class was the USS *Nimitz*, which entered service in 1975. Nine other Nimitz Class carriers followed – *Dwight D. Eisenhower* in 1977, *Carl Vinson*, *Theodore Roosevelt* and *Abraham Lincoln* during the 1980s,

*George Washington*, *John C. Stennis* and *Harry S. Truman* in the 1990s and *Ronald Reagan* and *George H.W. Bush* between 2003 and 2006. The long gap between batches of vessels was to allow the navy to plan the phased decommissioning of some of its older super carriers. These powerful warships – the largest of their kind in the world – can carry as many as 90 modern aircraft, but most deploy a 'carrier wing' of 64 assorted aircraft, the current range including F/A-18A Hornets, F/A-18E Super Hornets and EA-6B Prowlers.

While there are minor differences between the first three Nimitz Class carriers and those that followed them, the US Navy regard them as one composite class of warships. After 2000 it was decided to develop a new class of super carrier to replace the older Nimitz Class vessels. The first of these three Gerald R. Ford Class carriers will enter service in 2016, when *Nimitz* is due to be decommissioned after 41 years of service

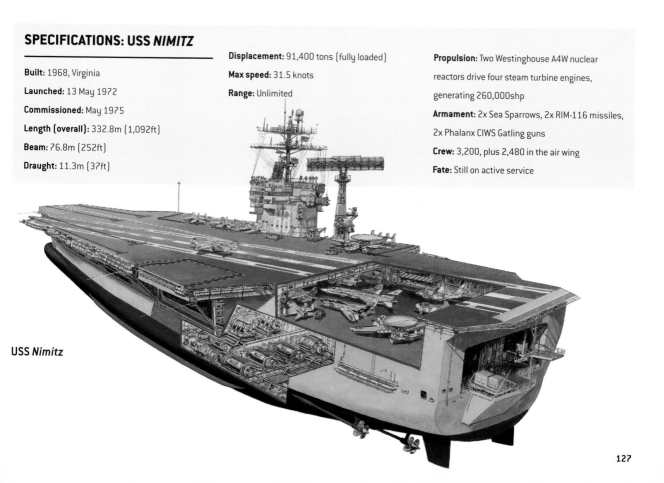

# SPECIFICATIONS: USS *NIMITZ*

**Built:** 1968, Virginia

**Launched:** 13 May 1972

**Commissioned:** May 1975

**Length (overall):** 332.8m (1,092ft)

**Beam:** 76.8m (252ft)

**Draught:** 11.3m (37ft)

**Displacement:** 91,400 tons (fully loaded)

**Max speed:** 31.5 knots

**Range:** Unlimited

**Propulsion:** Two Westinghouse A4W nuclear reactors drive four steam turbine engines, generating 260,000shp

**Armament:** 2x Sea Sparrows, 2x RIM-116 missiles, 2x Phalanx CIWS Gatling guns

**Crew:** 3,200, plus 2,480 in the air wing

**Fate:** Still on active service

USS *Nimitz*

# Ship details

**Previous page:** One of the largest and most powerful warships in the world, for almost four decades *Nimitz* and her embarked air group have projected American power around the globe. She has seen action off Iran (1979), Libya (1981), Lebanon (1985), Kuwait (1991), Iraq (2003) and the Indian Ocean, when she conducted sorties over Afghanistan (2009). The first of a nuclear-powered generation of carriers, *Nimitz* is due to be decommissioned after 2016.

**This page:** Launched in 2001 and commissioned in 2003, the *Ronald Reagan* is the ninth Nimitz Class nuclear-powered super carrier to enter service with the US Navy. Like other later carriers of the class she employs better flight deck protection than her predecessors, and better anti-submarine sensors. A more noticeable improvement is that her island was designed differently from the other ships of her class. She will remain in service until at least 2050.

USS *Ronald Reagan*